Exploring the INTERNET

Using Critical Thinking Skills

A SELF-PACED WORKBOOK FOR LEARNING
TO EFFECTIVELY USE THE INTERNET AND
EVALUATE ONLINE INFORMATION

DEBRA JONES

Neal-Schuman Publishers, Inc.

New York

London

Netscape Communications Corporation has not authorized, sponsored, or endorsed, or approved this publication and is not responsible for its content. Netscape and the Netscape Communications Corporate Logos, are trademarks and trade names of Netscape Communications Corporation. All other product names and/or logos are trademarks of their respective owners.

Published by Neal-Schuman Publishers, Inc.
100 Varick Street
New York, NY 10013

Library of Congress Cataloging-in-Publication Data

Jones, Debra.
   Exploring the Internet using critical thinking skills : a self-paced workbook for learning to effectively use the Internet and evaluate online information / by Debra Jones.
       p.   cm.
   Includes bibliographical references and index.
   ISBN 1–55570–319–4
   1. Computer network resources—United States—Problems, exercises, etc. 2. Critical thinking—United States—Problems, exercises, etc.
I. Title.
ZA4201.J66   1998
025.04—dc21   97–37139
                                                                    CIP

TABLE OF CONTENTS

COURSE GOAL

> To acquire information literacy for lifelong learning by developing critical thinking skills and applying them to Internet navigation and evaluation techniques.

COURSE OBJECTIVES

- Student will be able to define, identify, and locate Internet information sources.

- Student will be able to evaluate the usefulness and relevance of Internet information sources.

- Student will be able to identify, analyze, and evaluate evidence, assumptions, and logical arguments in information sources.

- Student will be able to identify bias, manipulative use of information, and personal opinion in an information source.

- Student will be able to apply appropriate citation styles and understand the basic responsibilities of online publishing.

MAP OF THE WORKBOOK

The Internet and the World Wide Web

CAVEATS TO THE LEARNER

- The entire online world is just too vast for us to present in entirety in the course of this instruction. It's growing faster than we can put this handbook together. We don't promise to cover it all.

- We do promise an integrated approach focusing on the process of seeking information and the value it brings to you.

- We include technical explanations and procedures in the lessons only when they are required to investigate or retrieve necessary information.

"Then how do I find out all there is to know about the Internet?"

1. Sign up for a computer course that will include computer management procedures.
2. Go to a bookstore or library and get one of the *many* books on computer skills and/or the Internet.

The technical procedures included are in a constant state of change. One thing you can be sure of is that as soon as you have something figured out, the procedures will change, usually for the better.

- Sometimes access to computer resources is limited. Make sure that you read the lessons ahead of time to maximize your online time.

SYMBOLS USED IN THE WORKBOOK

Throughout the lessons, you will see the following symbols. They will alert you to the process that is under way.

CONCEPTS

Concepts are general principles that you must understand in order to find information on the Internet.

DEFINITIONS

Definitions explain terms you need to know. Check the glossary in the back of the book for any other terms with which you may be unfamiliar.

TOOLS

Tools show you how to complete a procedure required in a practice exercise. There are many tools (for example, computer applications or search strategies) available when doing online research. However, we will be explaining only those tools necessary to perform a specific task.

PRACTICE

Practice is your chance to use the tools and concepts that have just been introduced. The lessons are structured to help you prepare by reading the exercises offline in order to maximize your time when practicing online.

INTRODUCING NETSCAPE

Throughout this workbook, Netscape will be the navigator for your travels on the Internet. This page introduces you to Netscape, one of the popular **browsers** for the **World Wide Web**. (Look in the glossary in the back for definitions of bolded terms. They will also be explained during the course of the workbook.) Other browsers you might use (for example, Microsoft Internet Explorer) are similar to Netscape in their basic navigation methods.

In order to access the Internet, your computer needs to be connected to either a local area network of computers (at your campus or workplace this may be called an *Intranet*) and then linked to the Internet, or via a modem and phone line to an Internet service provider. Our lessons begin with the assumption that you already are connected to the Internet either through an Intranet or by using your modem and phone line from home. (Our final lesson, Lesson 8, briefly describes the process of getting an Internet connection from your home.)

When you sit down at a computer running Netscape, your screen should look something like this. Examine this sample page for your first introduction to Netscape .

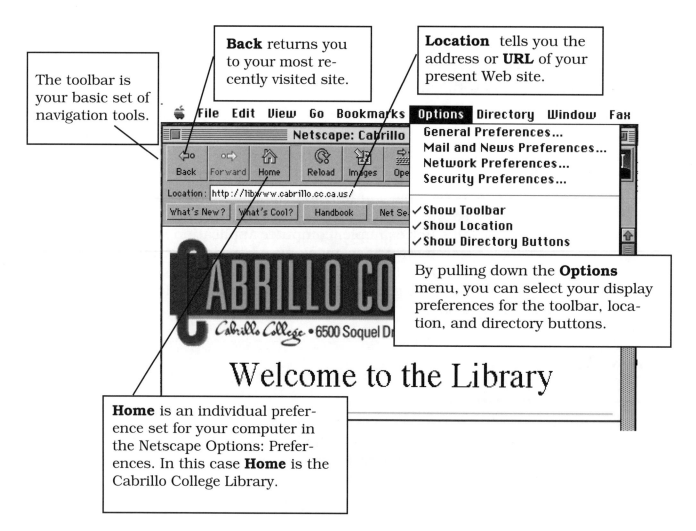

Back returns you to your most recently visited site.

Location tells you the address or **URL** of your present Web site.

The toolbar is your basic set of navigation tools.

By pulling down the **Options** menu, you can select your display preferences for the toolbar, location, and directory buttons.

Home is an individual preference set for your computer in the Netscape Options: Preferences. In this case **Home** is the Cabrillo College Library.

LESSON ONE: WALKING ONTO THE WEB

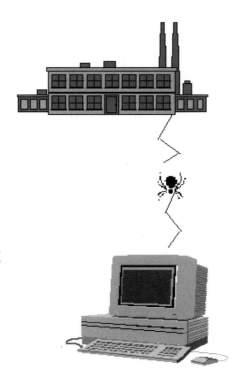

We all have heard the expression that we live in an "Information Age." The Industrial Age, from the mid 18th century into the early 20th century, produced largely manufactured goods. Information is now being mass produced, at mindbending speed. Information as we know it today—whether it is printed, electronically published, or broadcast via the media—will double in less than five years. The sum total of what we've learned in the last 30 years equals what was learned over the previous 5,000 years! The total of all printed knowledge doubles every eight years (Wurman 44). Analysts predict that by the year 2000, nearly all new information will be available first in digital form.

Let's look at some definitions. What is this "information" that overwhelms our lives now? Where does it come from? What is it good for? How do we use it effectively?

On the most basic level, information allows us to survive. Consider prehistoric man. Knowing where herds of animals lurked and knowing the local weather patterns both contributed to early man's survival. Today, survival means that two-thirds of all jobs tomorrow will be in an information-related capacity.

DEFINITIONS

Webster's Third New International Dictionary tells us that information is the communication or reception of knowledge or intelligence. It is the process through which an object or knowledge is impressed upon the mind that brings about a state of knowing. Through reception and "impression," information becomes knowledge. Sounds a bit like learning doesn't it?

Where does information come from? Information comes from data being transferred. Data, "something that is given from being experientially encountered or from being admitted or assumed for specific purposes" (Webster's 577), comes from scientists, researchers, and other observers. We can get information from our own world of sources; indeed, from anywhere in our world.

CONCEPTS

We can conceive of five rings of information surrounding us. Central to us is the internal information of our own reactions to our environment. Surrounding that is "conversational" information, which we pick up around us. "Reference" information is the next ring, the materials where we can seek out the systems of our world, from a cookbook to a telephone book to an encyclopedia. The fourth ring is "News & Media," which is transferred to us via the media. Our "Cultural Information"—history, philosophy, the arts, and our attempts to understand and put meaning into our civilization—comprise the final ring (Wurman 43).

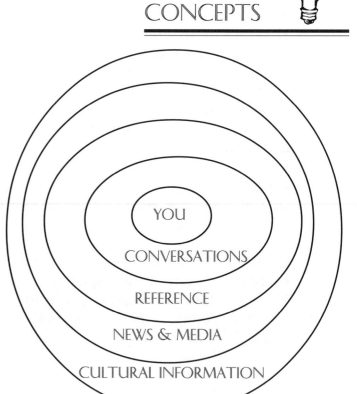

More information does not necessarily lead to a better or more satisfying life. Nor does it even lead to a more "knowledgeable" existence. Just as too much food can lead to gluttony, or as with any other substance abuse, a surfeit of information won't make us "smarter." Information overload can make us anxious. It has been argued that drowning ourselves in information is actually crippling in that we become incapable of differentiating the meaningful from the meaningless; thus any true value is lost. Think about how many instruction manuals you've chosen to ignore, how many news articles on world crises you've not been able to find time to read, and how many consumer reports you have bypassed (and then bought the item anyway)!

Nobel laureate economist Herbert Simon (1995) points out:

What information consumes is rather obvious: it consumes the attention of its recipients. Hence a wealth of information creates a poverty of attention, and a need to allocate that attention efficiently among the overabundance of information sources that might consume it (Simon 201).

This workbook charts a pathway through the morass of online information by introducing tools and concepts that will help you identify valuable information.

HOW'S THE WEATHER?

Everybody talks about the weather. Weather itself is information because it communicates raw observational data. We live with the knowledge of its effects, from "spring fever" to hurricanes and drought. Using the concept of the five rings of information just presented, identify how information about weather can come to us by listing on each of the five lines below one example of an information source about weather that is available to you.

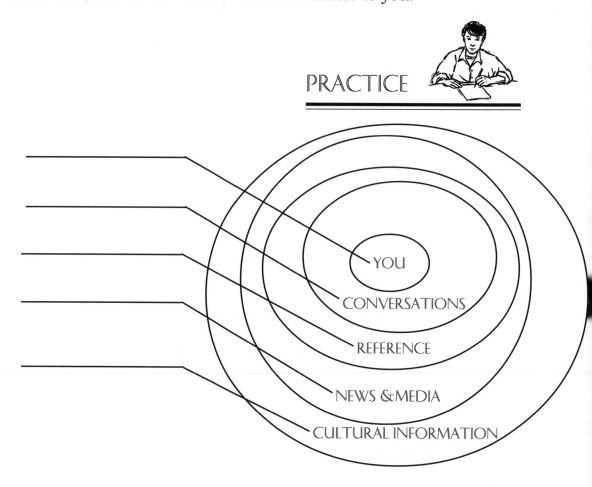

PRACTICE

YOU

CONVERSATIONS

REFERENCE

NEWS & MEDIA

CULTURAL INFORMATION

It would be reasonable to expect any of us to know about the weather. Look outside. Call a friend or check a weather map to find out weather in a distant location. One can locate weather statistics and trends from reference books. The online world offers us another option, one that brings us a bit more media and interactivity. But before we visit a weather site on the Internet, we need to be "informed" of some tools and definitions.

DEFINITIONS

Internet – The Internet describes the worldwide network of computers. The word *Internet* literally means "network of networks." The Internet is comprised of thousands of smaller regional networks throughout the world. Estimates vary widely as to the number of Internet users in the United States, ranging from 10 to 42 million. Trends indicate that whatever the number, Internet use doubles every 12 to 16 months.

World Wide Web – The World Wide Web is used on the Internet; but the Internet and the Web are not the same thing. The Web refers to a body of information—an abstract space of connected knowledge—and the Internet refers to the physical side of the global network, the connectivity provided by millions of cables and computers.

The World Wide Web was born in March 1989, when Tim Berners-Lee of the European Particle Physics Laboratory (also known as CERN) proposed a system of using networked hypertext (computer text links to other documents) for transmission of documents and communication among members across the Internet.

URL (Uniform Resource Locator) – URLs are the recognized way to give the address of any resource on the Internet that is part of the World Wide Web.

A URL might look like this:

	http://www.matisse.net/seminars.html
or	**telnet://well.sf.ca.us**
or	**gopher://liberty.uc.wlu.edu/11/gophers/**

 The first part of the URL specifies the method of access or Internet protocol. The following part is typically the address of the computer where the data or service is located. Further parts may specify the names of files, the connecting computer port, or the online textual database. URLs are always written as a single unbroken line with no spaces.

URLs generally begin with one of the following protocols, followed by a colon and two forward slashes. **Protocols** are the specifications or standards that computers use to recognize and communicate with each other.

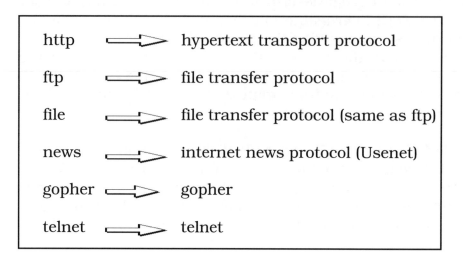

http	⟹	hypertext transport protocol
ftp	⟹	file transfer protocol
file	⟹	file transfer protocol (same as ftp)
news	⟹	internet news protocol (Usenet)
gopher	⟹	gopher
telnet	⟹	telnet

In general, the computer domain name (or address) that is the **server** for the information follows the two slashes (//).

The URL often can allow the researcher to identify the source of a document or service on the Internet. Just as you can identify the publisher of a book by looking at the title page or the producer of a movie by reading the movie credits, the URL identifies the *site*, or publishing location, of specific information on the Internet. Let's take a minute to dissect one.

Components of the URL are as follows:

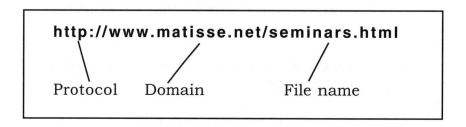

http://www.matisse.net/seminars.html

Protocol   Domain   File name

HTTP (Hypertext transport protocol) – HTTP is the **protocol**, or standard procedure, which moves the hypertext files across the Internet. HTTP requires an HTTP **client** computer program on one end and an HTTP **server** computer program on the other end. HTTP is the most important protocol used on the World Wide Web (WWW).

Hyperlinks – Hyperlinks are text or images that contains "links" to other documents. These links are usually words or phrases in the document that are different colors and underlined, although images can also serve as hyperlinks. A reader clicks one of these hot links to retrieve and display another document, located on that computer or at a remote location.

In the example at the bottom of page 6, the Internet protocol was HTTP, the communications protocol designed for the Web. The Web can handle all Internet protocols, however, so URLs might begin with other prefixes, such as gopher, telnet, or ftp.

A URL for a gopher site might look like this:

gopher://gopher.msu.ed/standards

Protocol   Domain   File name

Gopher – Gopher is a very successful method of making menus of computerized information available over the Internet. Gopher spread rapidly across the Internet, but is now largely being replaced by hypertext. There are still thousands of gopher servers on the Internet, and we can expect they will remain for a while.

Why Is It Named Gopher?

The Gopher program was written at the University of Minnesota. They named it for the industrious little animal scurrying about, using the name as a pun on "go fer" because it goes for your files. The fact that the gopher is the mascot of University of Minnesota might have had something to do with it too.

Domain name - The domain name is the structured, alphabetic-based, unique name for a computer on a network. Each computer also has a numeric Internet Protocol (IP) name. Either name can be used, but domain names tend to be easier to remember.

Example: **128.04.12.62**   or   **www.lib.uma.edu**

Domain names always have two or more parts, separated by dots. The part on the extreme left is the most specific, and the part on the extreme right is the most general; sometimes called the *top level.* Top-level domains are identified by three letter abbreviations and can give you a fairly good idea of where a document on the Internet is stored. Consider the following list:

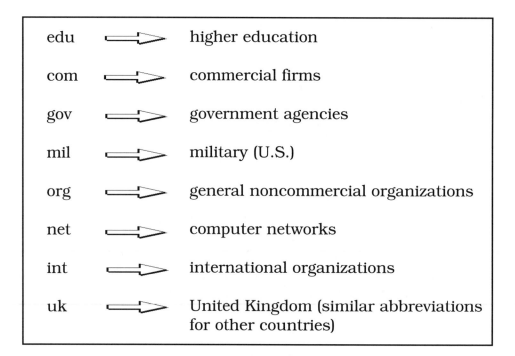

edu	higher education
com	commercial firms
gov	government agencies
mil	military (U.S.)
org	general noncommercial organizations
net	computer networks
int	international organizations
uk	United Kingdom (similar abbreviations for other countries)

Sometimes domain names will use a geographic hierarchy instead, for example:

www.cabrillo.cc.ca.us

web.school.community college.california. united states

Let's get back to talking about the weather. Your first stop is to find out about the weather, at any location, by going to a site called "Weather and Climate."

You know from the previous discussion about URLs that there are specific areas that you can identify. For practice, name each section as indicated:

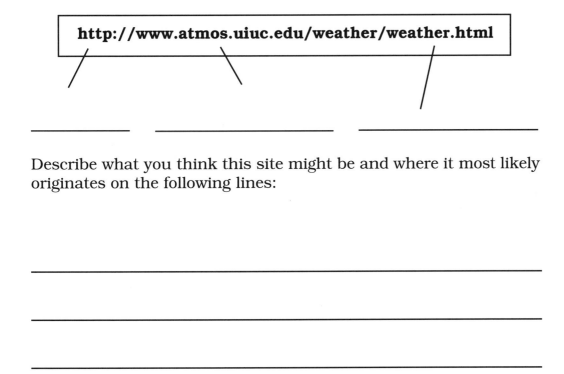

http://www.atmos.uiuc.edu/weather/weather.html

_____   _____   _____

Describe what you think this site might be and where it most likely originates on the following lines:

_____

_____

_____

Netscape is one of the most popular software programs, or browsers, used to navigate the Internet. However, any Internet browser that you use (for example, Netscape, Internet Explorer, Lynx, or the browser in America Online) includes a spot for you to type in the URL. Regardless of what page you find on Netscape when you start, you should see a menu bar across the top of the screen. (If the menu bar is not available, adjust the Options, as mentioned in the introductory page "Introducing Netscape.") Now click on the **Open** button.

After you click on **Open**, type in the URL for the "Weather and Climate" site:

http://www.atmos.uiuc.edu/weather/weather.html

Be careful to type it exactly as shown! Any misplaced letter or symbol will bring up an error message.

Did you get there? If not, check your spelling and make sure that there are no spaces between the letters. If you still have no luck, check with a librarian or fellow student to see whether he or she can spot the problem. Once there, examine the entire page. What are your initial impressions of this first site? What is your opinion?

_____

_____

_____

_____

NEXT STOP: THE WEATHER ~ UP CLOSE!

What's the weather like in your own area? Try this site:

http://www.earthcam.com

The EarthCam site is a directory of live indoor and outdoor Internet cameras focused on a variety of subjects. Select the category **Weather** and try to find a weather camera in your general location. (If there is not one from your area, just select one of interest to you.)

How's the weather at this site? Does it match your own information on the topic? You too are an expert on this topic. Tell us what the information at this weather site tells you, and then compare it to your own information. What are the differences? How do you account for them?

_____

_____

_____

_____

_____

_____

_____

LESSON TWO: THE CRITICAL THINKER

You can start your Internet research with the weather because it is straightforward data, accessible to anyone with a thermometer, barometer, or rain gauge. We all could be considered experts in the weather. You might find that the weatherperson on your favorite TV channel has about the same success rate in forecasting the weather as you do!

CONCEPTS

Why use the weather to think about critical thinking on the Internet? Consider this: of all the topics we could talk about, become "informed" about, or offer an opinion on, what could be more free of hidden personal bias or assumptions than our physical environment? Certainly we might disagree whether the hot weather is pleasant or not, or whether it's good that it rained every day this week, but we can all be observation "experts."

If we return to the idea of how information comes to us, we know that the central core is our own perception, our own awareness of our environment. What we "know" is our implicit personal knowledge, or our assumptions and beliefs about our world. For example, if it is getting darker outside, I can assume that either it is dusk or that perhaps it's going to rain. When it gets darker outside, I don't need to consult another source of information, I already "know" the reason. I may take action such as turning on a light as a result.

You are thinking critically when you are actively thinking *about* your thinking. You are examining your assumptions from your most implicit personal knowledge to the most abstract level of impersonal information coming to you from any possible source. Your implicit assumptions (that when it becomes dark outside it is most likely dusk) are how you structure and filter the information you receive. The process of making explicit, or examining and justifying, your assumptions is the basic action involved in critical thinking. If my basic assumption does not match other verifiable facts (that is, it is 1:00 p.m., so it must not be dusk) then as a critical thinker I question my original assumptions and seek other evidence. This process of analyzing assumptions following a logical sequence of thoughts and looking for alternative explanations is the "work" of a critical thinker.

DEFINITIONS

John Dewey, often called the father of modern education, defined critical thinking as "active, persistent, and careful consideration of any belief or supposed form of knowledge in the light of the grounds that support it [in a] conscious and voluntary effort to establish belief upon a firm basis of evidence and rationality" (Dewey 9).

Other contemporary educators have described critical thinking as "reflective and reasonable thinking that is focused on deciding what to believe or do" (Ennis 45), and "the intellectually disciplined process of actively and skillfully conceptualizing, applying, analyzing, synthesizing, and/or evaluating information gathered from, or generated by, observation, experience, reflection, reasoning, or communication, as a guide to belief and action" (Scriven and Paul 1).

CONCEPTS

The researcher embarking on a search through the maze of today's online information world needs to be armed with a critical mind. Many of the assumptions about information delivery are no longer valid because now anyone with a computer and a modem can publish. Prepublication screening and editorial review is not the standard in the Internet as it is in the print world. Anyone who puts up a personal home page has the same exposure as a large, established publisher. Publication on the Internet is not limited to credible, verifiable sources, bearing the stamp of reputable publishers. Nor does marketplace value drive online publications, because most everything posted on the Internet is free.

The source of the information and the credibility of that source are much harder to discern online than through traditional print or media modes. No requirements or accepted standards are in place for identifying or presenting online material. Critical thinking skills and an active and questioning mind are needed to judge the veracity and credibility of online sources.

PRACTICE

Click on **Open** and enter this URL:

http://cirrus.sprl.umich.edu/WUnderground/UM-WEATHER.html

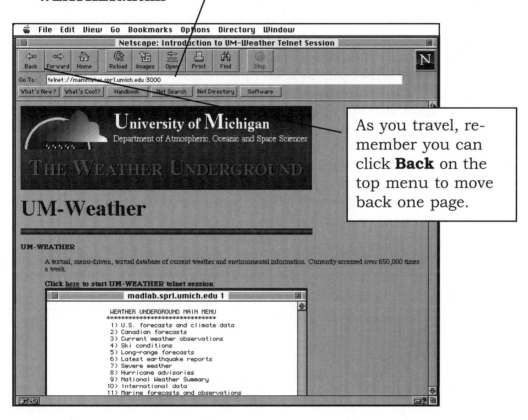

As you travel, remember you can click **Back** on the top menu to move back one page.

As you read through the UM-WEATHER site, which agencies do you find are responsible for sponsoring this site?

_____

_____

What are your assumptions about the reliability of the source of this weather information?

_____

_____

Generally, **hypertext** is any text that contains "links" to other documents—words or phrases in the document that can be chosen by a user and which cause another document to be retrieved and displayed. Using Netscape, you will see that one color of the highlighted links (often blue) will represent sites you have not yet visited, while ones you have been to in the recent past are a different color (often purple). The particular color and the length of time visited sites remain different colors are preferences that can be set individually on each computer.

Hypertext, which makes it possible for you to travel between documents or sites following your own order or path, is done through **HTML**, or **HyperText Markup Language**. HTML is the computer language used to create hypertext documents for use on the Web. Embedded in the code of the HTML are the directions and the **protocol** to access the document or site referred to in the linked text. Your computer, behind the scenes, interprets the hypertext and does the work to connect to that link. If you want to get a look at the HTML source code, you can open the **View** menu and choose **Source** to see the document in HTML format.

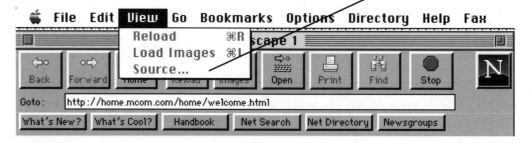

This source file with the hypertext markup language includes all the directions needed for your computer, using the applications included in Netscape, to travel the Internet and retrieve the information or document you have requested. To go back to your hypertext document, open the **File** menu and choose **Quit**.

What are your impressions of the HTML source code behind the hypertext document you just examined?

_____

_____

Here is a sample of HTML source code for the UM-WEATHER page:

```
<head> <title>Introduction to UM-Weather Telnet Session</title> </head>
<body>
<A NAME="Contents"><IMG SRC="../graphics/Wunderground.gif"></A>
<H1><FONT SIZE="+5">UM-Weather</FONT></H1>
<IMG SRC="../graphics/BlueLine.gif">
<DL>
<DT><A NAME="UM-WEATHER"><STRONG>UM-WEATHER</STRONG></A><p>
<DD>A textual, menu-driven, textual database of current weather and
environmental information.  Currently accessed over 650,000 times a
week.<p>
<STRONG>Click <A HREF="telnet://mammatus.sprl.umich.edu:3000">here</A>
to start UM-WEATHER telnet session</STRONG>
```

This is the command language telling your computer to use the protocol **telnet** to the hypertext link at the University of Michigan.

This shows as the blue or purple highlighted hypertext link on your Netscape screen.

PRACTICE

Access weather information by clicking on the highlighted text at this University of Michigan Web site: "Click **here** to start UM-WEATHER telnet session."

The screen now looks different. Netscape launched the application **telnet** to connect your computer to the computer that serves up the weather information.

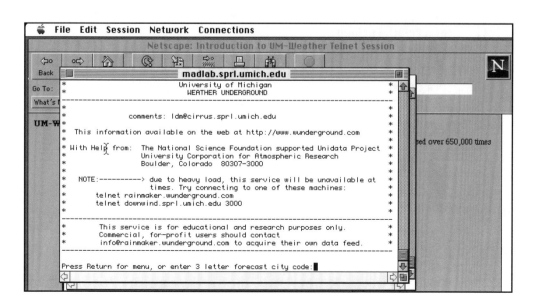

DEFINITIONS

Telnet – Telnet is the software program that allows you to log into remote computer systems on the Internet. The computer that you log into is often referred to as the *remote host*. When you telnet to another computer, you are using the computing resources on the other end. Your computer actually becomes a "dumb" terminal and does not rely on its own computing power. You will be affected by any slow time or down time that the remote system is experiencing. When you are connected via telnet to another computer, you can access whatever services that remote machine is providing to its local machines.

Telnet has been a common way for Internet users to search library systems at distant locations. There are a number of telnet commands, but the basic ones users need to know are the commands given in the first screen when you reach the host computer. Typing **quit** generally allows you to leave the host computer, and opening the **File** menu and choosing **Quit** allows you to quit your telnet connection.

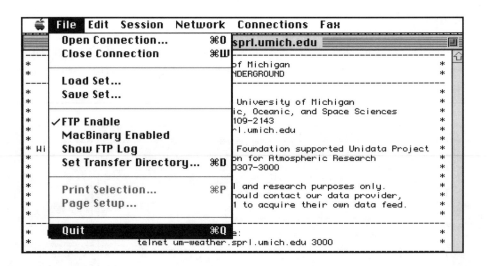

Due to space limitations, we will not be able to cover the telneting application thoroughly in this lesson. For more information, check out books on the Internet in libraries or bookstores, or try this source:

http://www.clark.net/pub/lschank/explore/telnet.html

PRACTICE

Now that you have looked at the original producer of the information for the UM-WEATHER site, what clues would you use to evaluate its reliability and usefulness?

_____

_____

_____

How do you compare this site to Weather and Climate and the local site you visited in Lesson 1 for weather information? Which do you prefer and why?

_____

_____

_____

As a new Internet surfer, give us a few of your thoughts about the Internet and about your travels on the Internet so far. Is it what you expected? Why or why not?

_____

_____

_____

LESSON THREE: EVALUATING SOURCES

As an online researcher, you need to keep three elements at the top of your mind: assumptions, evidence, and logic. In this lesson, we will examine the evidence, look for credible sources, and evaluate the assumptions and logic in the material presented.

It is important for critical thinkers travelling in an online world to practice the following skills. As we introduce each of the following lessons, we will refer again to the specific critical thinking skills emphasized in that lesson. These skills are indicated by the arrows in the boxes like the one below.

> ⇒ Differentiate between fact and opinion.
> Examine assumptions, including your own.
> Be flexible and open-minded as you look for explanations, causes, and solutions to problems.
>
> ⇒ Be aware of fallacious arguments, ambiguity, and manipulative reasoning.
> Stay focused on the whole picture, while examining the specifics.
>
> ⇒ Look for reputable sources.

CONCEPTS

The online world presents a different set of challenges to the researcher than those in the print world. Books and journals will reveal the author, the publisher, and the date of the material readily on the first pages of the publication. Sources you discover on the Internet do not follow these conventions. The source of the information, the date, and the purpose of the online presentation are often hard to determine. Once the basic background on the source of the information has been located, the researcher will need to consider many criteria to discern its usefulness and credibility. These same criteria should be used in evaluating the credibility of any source of information—print, online, or personal.

EVALUATION OF WEB RESOURCES

Use these criteria to help you determine the credibility of information sources:

Source: Can you easily identify the creator of the page of information? Responsible online publication should give the source of the information in a readily visible place on the page. Does the source give their affiliation, credentials, or reason for publishing the information? A source may very likely state its aim in the initial presentation. This is often preferable to a "hidden agenda." Be aware that the individual author or Web designer of a page (such as E.T. Schmoo) could be listed, while the source of the information is actually an institution, association, or other larger entity (for example, the Center for Exploration of Online Phenomenon).

Credentials: See whether you can discover, by looking over the information, what the author's credentials are. What is the author's background and why does this make him or her an expert? With which institution or group is the author affiliated? Is the affiliation with an impartial group or a group established to promote an idea or point of view (like the National Rifle Association)?

Type of information: Is the information scholarly (produced by researchers in the field), popular (produced for the general public), governmental, from a private business or association, or basically an advertisement for the author's product or service? Web pages often fall into one of the following categories: entertainment, educational, business, individual personal pages, or informative. Think of the differences you might find in pages presented by www.billybob.com compared to www.audubon.org.

Purpose: Try to discern whether the author is making an argument for personal gain (selling a point of view), offering an opinion (a commentary written by an authority in the field is still an opinion), giving a factual report (news items), or relaying personal observation. Look to see whether you can identify objective writing (presenting both sides fairly) or a subjective bias (expressing one's own point of view).

Sources: Where did the author gather the information presented? Was it from original research, experiments, observation, interviews, books, and documents? Does the author or publisher provide references to locate the original sources of the information? Keep in mind the author's assumptions, or the reasons behind why the author is providing the information.

Timeliness: When and where was the material published? Does it consider the topic in a relevant and current manner? Far too often Web pages are published and never updated. Look carefully for a date, and don't be misled into thinking that the online version is necessarily more current than the print version.

Style: An author can present information to you in a clear, reasonable, and orderly argument. Or the same information can be presented in an obtuse or illogical manner. Seek out information that is accessible to you and that is useful to your level of research. Be aware that an author's style (humorous, overly complex, boring, etc.) can prejudice your perception of the information.

Assumptions: The perspective of the writer, or point of view, makes certain assumptions about you the reader. Be aware that these assumptions about you are unsubstantiated opinion. Many fallacious arguments can be built on what the author assumes both you and he "believe" to be true. For example, a page on teaching cats to talk might assume that we all "know" that cats are the smartest animals around.

For more information on evaluation of sources, check out the following Web pages:

> **http://www.science.widener.edu/~withers/webeval.htm**
> "Teaching Critical Evaluation Skills for World Wide Web Resources" from the Widener University

> **http://infopeople.berkeley.edu:8000/bkmk/select.html**
> "Evaluating Internet Resources: A checklist"

> **http://thorplus.lib.purdue.edu/library_info/instruction/ gs175/3gs175/evaluation.html**
> "Evaluating World Wide Web Information"

> **http://alexia.lis.uiuc.edu/~janicke/Evaluate.html**
> Janicke, Lisa. "Resource selection and information evaluation."

> **http://urisref.library.cornell.edu/skill26.htm**
> Ormondroyd, Joan, Michael Engle, and Tony Cosgrave. "How to critically analyze information sources."

> **http://www.tiac.net/users/hope/findqual.html**
> Tillman, Hope. "Evaluating quality on the Net."

Sometimes researchers feel that trying to find information on the Web is like walking into a library after an earthquake, with the books strewn all over the floor. On the other hand, with the appropriate tools, you can locate information precisely, just as if you could pick the one paragraph you need out of all those books in disarray on the library floor, without having to open a single one.

But how do you find information on the Internet? The various search applications utilize somewhat different approaches. Using Netscape, click once on the menu button Net Search.

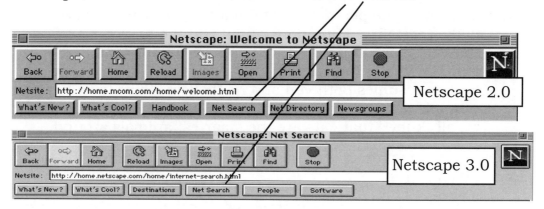

Netscape provides links to the major search engines from their Net Search page. Net Search alternates the search engine that is displayed first. Below the first search engine, you will find links to other search engines.

You can reach Infoseek directly by entering its URL in the Open box:

http://guide.infoseek.com/

TOOLS

INFOSEEK

This example shows a search done with the search engine Infoseek. Most search engines use crawlers—spider programs that automatically travel the Internet, following document links and collecting and indexing information such as the URL, document title, and keywords in the document.

Search engines vary in the extent of the Web that they index. Most index Web pages, Usenet newsgroups articles, Gopher menus, and ftp sites. They also vary in the search capabilities offered and are not uniform or standard in search strategies. Begin searching by entering the keywords you believe should appear in the sources you seek.

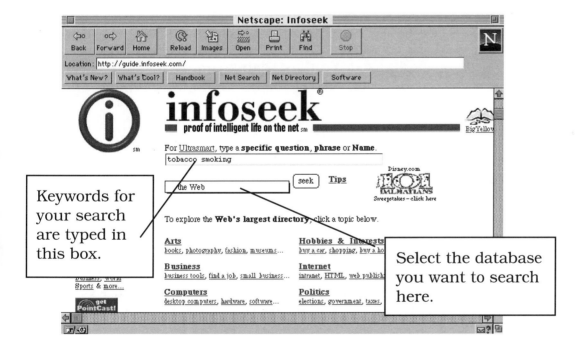

The search engine will return a list of "hits," or sites that have a high likelihood of being relevant to your topic because your search words appeared either in greater frequency or in more primary positions than other sites. Simple searching can be done by using well-defined key terms and using a few of the following search hints. For more advanced searching tips, it's a good idea to read through the individual search engine's "search tips" or "advanced searching" sections.

SEARCH HINTS

Use the following hints to help you search more effectively:

⟹ Select unique words and phrases that are likely to appear in the documents you want to find. Check your search statement for misspelled words and typographical errors.

⟹ Use the capitalization you expect to find in the target documents. Capitalized words will usually be searched as proper names, lowercase words will be searched as both proper and not. Example: **apple** will find the fruit and the company.

⟹ Identify phrases by surrounding them with double quotation marks or by hyphenating the words in the phrases. Example: "right of way," right-of-way (no spaces between the words)

⟹ You can join your keywords by using the boolean operators AND and OR. Some search engines require that these words be capitalized. You also can structure searches by grouping words using parentheses. Example: (whales OR cetaceans) AND migration.

⟹ Most search engines assume that you are doing an OR boolean search (see next page). When you list keywords, results will include **any** of the words you list, not necessarily **all**. Using the boolean operator OR implies that any of the keywords you list will satisfy the search. The boolean operator AND implies that all the keywords you list must be included. Look to see whether the search engine allows you to select to search for either all (AND) or any (OR) of the specified keywords. NOT will exclude that word. Example: (Apple AND computer) NOT fruit.

⟹ In most search engines, you can specify that a particular word **must** be in the results list by placing a plus sign (+) directly in front of the word (no spaces). Conversely, you can place a minus sign (–) directly in front of the word to exclude any occurrences. Example: apple + computer – fruit.

⟹ The results of your search are listed in order of relevance. For each document, you see a numerical score showing how well the document matches your search.

PRACTICE

VISUALIZING YOUR SEARCH

Before you go online, try mapping out your concepts. Use this map to help you select similar terms (ORs) that you will combine (ANDs) with other terms in the next columns to narrow your search. Look over this example:

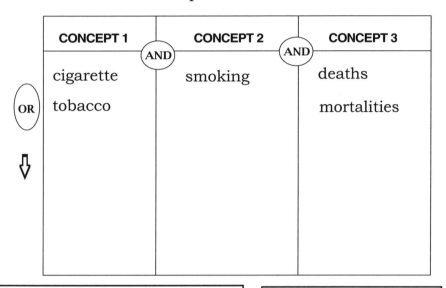

	CONCEPT 1		CONCEPT 2		CONCEPT 3
OR	cigarette tobacco	AND	smoking	AND	deaths mortalities

Boolean operator OR: This search will retrieve any documents with either FELONS or PRISONERS in the document.

Boolean operators AND and NOT: This search turns up college basketball but excludes any mentioning pro ball.

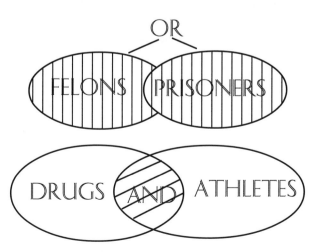

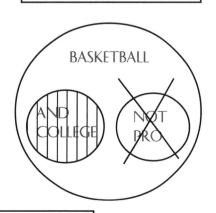

Boolean operator AND: This search will retrieve only documents containing both keywords DRUGS and ATHLETES.

In this search, we chose to look for information on the effects of smoking tobacco. To investigate the **number of deaths caused by tobacco**, you could type the keywords **tobacco smoking**, or any other choice of relevant keywords. After you click on the **Seek Now** button, Infoseek will come back with the first ten hits, or possibilities that match the words you entered.

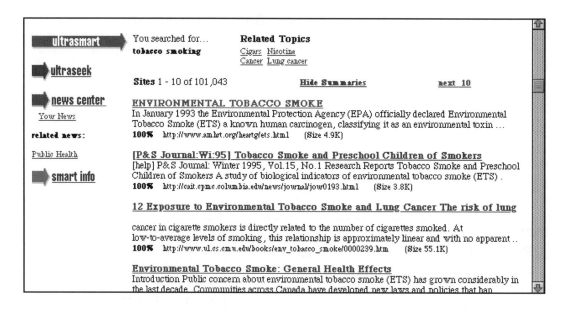

Scroll through the possibilities until you see a description of one that looks like it might provide valid evidence. Try to find one that will give you the necessary information to evaluate critically the author and source of the information. Scan the document to answer the following:

What keywords did you use? _____

Who is the author and/or source of the document you retrieved?

_____

_____

_____

Using the information evaluation guidelines given on pages 22-23, what do you know about the intended purpose of the document you retrieved?

_____

_____

What do you know about the credibility and/or authority of the author?

_____

_____

How would you evaluate the effectiveness or usability of the evidence you uncovered? Why?

_____

_____

_____

Find an example of the author's bias, point of view, or assumptions in reasoning. Describe it below.

_____

_____

_____

In the example used in this practice, we retrieved 101,043 possible sites—far too many for a searcher to review and evaluate. How might you improve this search to retrieve more accurate results which are more pertinent to our specific question?

_____

_____

_____

Now use Infoseek for a search using your own terms. Locate a
document that provides the necessary information to evaluate the
evidence presented, either positively or negatively. Explain below
what you found.

Describe your research question: _____

_____

_____

Search keywords used: _____

URL: _____

Author or publisher of the site: _____

Date of publication: _____

Purpose of the information: _____

_____

Your evaluation of its usefulness: _____

_____

_____

_____

_____

Try to find an example of bias, point of view, or assumptions in
reasoning in the source you uncovered. Describe it below.

_____

_____

_____

_____

LESSON FOUR: HOW WIDE IS THE WEB?

The Web is developing and changing so rapidly that getting an understanding of it is like shooting at a moving target.

Thus far you have looked at a few definitions and used a few tools to access the Web. As you look again at the attributes of the critical thinker listed below, remember that you need to examine your assumptions regarding the information's source and consider the evidence while you apply evaluation criteria to documents you retrieved via Infoseek and Veronica searches.

In this lesson these skills will be emphasized:

⟹ Be aware of fallacious arguments, ambiguity, and manipulative reasoning.

⟹ Stay focused on the whole picture, while examining the specifics.

For you as the researcher, to be able to utilize the available resource possibilities—online, print, or in person, you need to get a clear picture of what the Web is and what it can truly offer you. You easily can become lost in your travels on the Web, mindlessly moving from site to site. It is essential to keep in mind the sources of information and how and why information comes to be on the Web in order to accurately assess whether Web sources will be valuable and effective. Some information will never be located through online resources; some will be found only there. A few definitions will help paint the large picture of the Web.

DEFINITIONS

The World Wide Web is the global hypermedia-based system which allows access to the universe of Internet resources. The following list explores the basic concepts that make it work.

- The Web provides navigation based on hypertext, where users click on highlighted or underlined links to move to related pages of text or multimedia sources such as sound, images, or software.

- The Web uses programs, known as browsers, to allow individuals to "surf," or travel, the Web. Netscape is the browser used in this book, but there are others, such as Mosaic or Lynx (a browser that supports only text).

- Web browsers use a set of routines to tell your computer to search, retrieve, and display information in a variety of formats—text, images, sound, etc.

- Hypertext links enable you to access another page within the current document or on a file served by another computer anywhere that allows remote logins or data transfers from Internet users.

- While Gopher enables you to travel the Internet by providing you with a hierarchical and linear menu organization leading from folder (or menu) to documents, the Web allows nonlinear travel from document to document by using HTML (Hypertext Marked Language) to establish links between documents.

- The Web uses a URL as the unique address for any document on the Web. The HTML document has within it the commands needed to connect hypertext links and retrieve documents. Therefore, you do not need to use many computer commands to navigate the Web.

CONCEPTS

The researcher needs to understand both the concept and the tools needed to seek out information. The Web consists of the hypertext documents that have been created and made available on the Internet using client/server hardware and software (browsers such as Netscape) that allow you to retrieve and display the information.

Your quest in this exercise is to get the "whole picture." As an information seeker and evaluator, you should be able to select the most likely source or area for investigation of your topic. The Web is a gold mine, but you have to be realistic about what it offers.

INFORMATION STORAGE

3000 B.C.–
Clay tablets:
1 character per 1 cubic inch

1450 A.D.–
Printed page:
500 characters
per cubic inch

1990s –
Optical disk:
125,000,000,000
characters per cubic inch

*How big is the elephant?
How can we measure it and
use it for our purposes?*

The Web certainly is a bigger animal than man has ever seen before. Although it is a gigantic warehouse of information, you won't find everything there! Let's talk realistically about what information you'll find on the Internet and what you won't.

The amount of information available via the Internet is limitless. Anyone who has a computer connected to the Internet and wants to make his or her information available can publish. No restrictions, guidelines, or review procedures control contributions to the information pool. Educational institutions, businesses, non-profit organizations, governments, communities, and individual people all serve as information providers.

This sharing of resources and information is an example of collaboration and cooperation to extend the communication of information to anyone who wants to participate. The responsibility for the quality, accuracy, and timeliness of the contributed information remains with those same individuals and organizations, however, leading to unevenness in quality and quantity. The user of the information must judge the usefulness, accuracy, and reliablity of the information he or she uncovers. We have given you a few general guidelines for determining the value of information in earlier lessons. Use these clues, practice them, look with a critical eye, and be realistic about what information you might find, and consider where, why, and how it comes to be on the Internet.

Think logically, practically, and critically before you search the Internet for your information. Use these questions to prepare for your search:

 Does the information cost a lot of money in its printed form? Publishers have little motive to make expensive reference tools like encyclopedias and CD-ROM indexes available free of charge to the general public via the Internet.

 Is the information generally in demand? If the public would like to see the information available online, and if there are no financial limitations, chances are that someone has made the effort to get it online. Car prices from the *Kelley Blue Book* are now available online. The publisher of this popular and expensive reference source must believe it is worth the loss of subscriptions for the other benefits or income they receive from having it online.

 Will the information be available online? Some information is just never going to be online. So much has been published in the past (think of all those newpapers!) that if interest is not high it will probably remain only in print form. And, as experienced researchers know, there are many facts, fascinating as they may be, that just cannot be known (for example: the number of earthlings abducted by aliens never to be seen again!).

Will the information be helpful? What one person might consider information, someone else might not. Many online publishers consider their opinions and insights about the world to be worthy of general consumption. You and I probably won't hold that high an opinion of a lot of self-published pieces available on the Internet. As the saying goes, *caveat emptor*, or "let the buyer beware!"

PRACTICE

As critical thinkers, we try to get an idea of the whole picture. When we're talking about the whole world of information, that's a big whole.

This exercise is not online, but it requires you to think and plot your strategy as an information seeker both on and off the Internet. Given the descriptions of what you might and might not find, pick a new subject now that you want to explore.

Describe the research question:

_____

_____

What are some key words you would use to describe your search?

_____

Realizing that you are not yet an experienced online searcher, go ahead and make a guess about how successful a search on the Internet for your research topic might be. Explain why you feel this way:

_____

_____

_____

List some additional information sources and tools you would use that are not online resources. For example, if your research is on high school dropouts, you might also locate magazine articles using magazine indexes, or you might interview dropouts themselves.

_____

_____

_____

Reality Check – This part of the exercise requires a little collaboration with an "expert" or a fellow student. Find someone to read your answers to the preceding questions and have him jot down his impression of your possible research direction. For example, try asking a librarian, a fellow student in the library where you're working, your roommate, or someone you know who is "Internet savvy."

_____

_____

_____

_____

Once you have established that a search on the Internet might be worth a try, how do you go about locating documents and information relevant to your research topic? Thinking back to research in the traditional library, you know you could use the online catalog to find books. You also can use either print or CD-ROM indexes to search for magazine articles. What resources might you use?

_____

_____

CONCEPTS

In some ways, the online search world is very similar to the print world; finding information in both worlds requires using the appropriate tools. However, the Web is undergoing such rapid change that new resources and access tools evolve almost daily. A good Web explorer understands the basic concepts of online publishing, how the search engines work, and what sort of resources might be located in order to determine the best search approach.

In general, you can approach your information search by using either a full-text search engine (like Infoseek, which was used earlier) or a subject directory listing (like Yahoo, which you will use in the following exercise).

Subject listings of Internet resources are much like using a subject search approach for locating books in a library. Subject headings are predetermined by the indexers, which may be librarians when the books are cataloged or the Web indexers.

Some subject directories (such as Yahoo) are hierarchical menu systems with general categories that become more specific and a simple search feature. Web pages are indexed by subject, accessible through the subject directory by a series of qualifying choices.

One advantage of subject directories is that the sources included are submitted to indexers—real people who evaluate and select the resources. Many of the "empty" sites, the advertisements, or the personal pages won't be included in directories. The Web search engines we previously discussed gather and include all documents that they can retrieve. Subject listings of Web resources are different in this selective approach. When you use subject listings, you will get something related to the subject given and of some value, at least in the minds of the indexers.

PRACTICE

YAHOO

In this practice exercise, you will do a search using the oldest and best-known subject directory, Yahoo. Later you will compare it to a search using a Web search engine such as Infoseek. For this example, you are going to try to find some arguments in favor of hunting. By using a subject directory, you will become more focused by selecting progressively more specific subject headings. In this research query, defining effective keywords for a search engine would be difficult ("good" OR "pro" AND "hunting"?). Using the browsing approach of a subject directory will get you closer to your target.

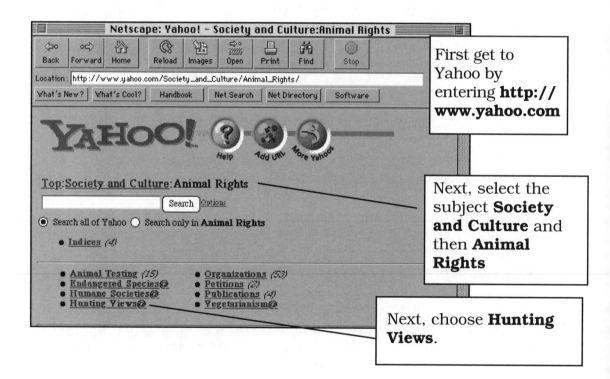

First get to Yahoo by entering **http://www.yahoo.com**

Next, select the subject **Society and Culture** and then **Animal Rights**

Next, choose **Hunting Views**.

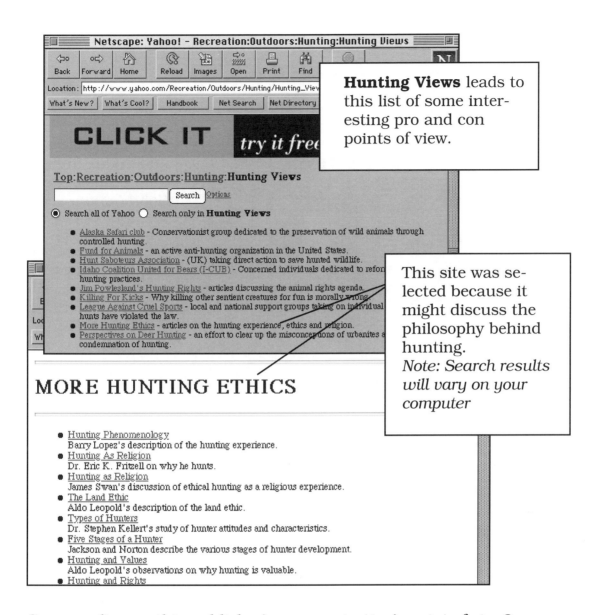

Can you discern this publisher's or organization's point of view?

_____

_____

Do you feel this site would be worth further investigation? Why or why not?

_____

_____

At this point, how do you think the research process could be improved?

_____

_____

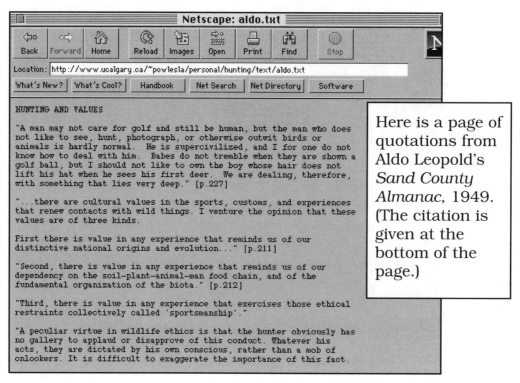

What is your opinion of this writer's point of view? Do you feel his arguments are persuasive or presented well? What assumptions does he make in his presentation?

_____

_____

_____

Do you feel that this source is valuable or applicable to the original research question? Why or why not?

_____

_____

_____

Did this example keep track of the whole picture, or did we get lost in our research? Can you suggest how the search might have been more successful?

_____

_____

_____

PRACTICE

Now it's your turn to follow your own research topic using Yahoo. Use a topic you've explored before, or select a new idea. State clearly your research purpose. What do you intend to find?

_____

_____

_____

With which source did you finish your subject browsing? Attach a printout if available. Give the URL, the author or publisher of the source, and any other pertinent information.

_____

_____

_____

Is your source reputable? Does it have validity in your research area? How did you judge this?

_____

_____

_____

How close did your end result come to answering your original research question? Were you able to stay focused and on track? Why or why not?

_____

_____

_____

_____

TOOLS

INTERNET SUBJECT DIRECTORIES

In addition to Yahoo, many other good subject guides to Web resources are available, and more are added all the time. Many libraries and other groups or individuals create their own favorite subject search directories and make them available on their home pages. Listed here are some general favorites:

- **A2Z – http://a2z.lycos.com/index.html**
  The top 10 percent of the most commonly linked sites

- **Argus Clearinghouse for Subject-oriented Internet Guides- http://www.clearinghouse.net/**
  Value-added topical guides which identify, describe, and evaluate Internet-based information systems

- **EINet Galaxy- http://www.einet.net/**
  Selections from the best of the Net

- **Internet Public Library Ready Reference Collection - http://ipl.sils.umich.edu:80/ref/RR/**
  References organized like a public library

- **WWW Virtual Library - http://www.w3.org/hypertext/DataSources/bySubject/**
  Distributed subject catalogue

- **Yahoo - http://www.yahoo.com/**
  The originator of the Internet subject directories

- **Yanoff's List - http://www.spectracom.com/islist/ inet2.html**
  Another extensive list of Internet resources

HOW MUCH OF THE WEB IS COVERED BY	
AltaVista	30 million pages
Excite	11.5 million pages
Infoseek	1 million pages
Open Text	1.6 million pages
Yahoo	80,000 pages

TOOLS

INTERNET SEARCH ENGINES

Both indexes and subject directories can help you find what you're looking for on the Internet. An index differs from a directory in that with an index you search for occurrences of a specific word or phrase. A directory lets you search for concepts or subject categories.

Search engines do the work of indexing the Internet. Internet "robots" or search engines comb the Web daily, indexing what they find. The search commands, range of resources covered, and search specifications differ somewhat among the indexes available. The speed, detail of returned information, and the extent to which you can specify search parameters might make one search engine more appealing to you than another. Some of the major search engines are listed here, with their URLs:

- **AltaVista - http://www.altavista.digital.com**
- **Excite - http://www.excite.com**
- **Hotbot - http://www.hotbot.com/index.html**
- **Infoseek - http://guide.infoseek.com**
- **Lycos - http://www.lycos.com**
- **WebCrawler - http://webcrawler.com/**

The proliferation of search engines has led to the creation of "meta" search tools. These search engines allow the user to search many of the most popular search engines simultaneously, using a single interface. Popular metasearch engines include:

- **Metacrawler - http://metacrawler.cs.washington.edu:8080/ index.html**
- **SavvySearch - http://guaraldi.cs.colostate.edu:2000/form**
- **DogPile - http://www.dogpile.com**

COMPARING INTERNET SEARCH ENGINES

The proliferation of search engines also has led to some valiant and intelligent comparative analyses of their relative advantages and disadvantages. It isn't as simple as asking, "What's your favorite search engine?" Due to the competitive nature of the Web, similarities abound and individual limitations are corrected rapidly. A critical thinker considers which search engine will best fit her search needs. It is very important to review the "Search Hints" or online help pages provided with any search engine. The online search tutorials listed here can give you more information on the individual features of search engines:

- **Choose the Best Search Engine for Your Information Needs -**
  http://www.nueva.pvt.k12.ca.us/~debbie/library/research/adviceengine.html

- **Web Search Tool Features -**
  http://www.unn.ac.uk/features.htm

- **Internet Search Tool Details -**
  http://sunsite.berkeley.edu/Help/searchdetails.html

- **Search Engine Watch -**
  http://searchenginewatch.com/

- **Sink or Swim: Internet Search Tools & Techniques -**
  http://oksw01.okanagan.bc.ca/libr/connect96/search.htm

- **The Search Is Over -**
  http://www.zdnet.com/pccomp/features/fea1096/sub2.html

- **CNET reviews - where to find anything on the Net -**
  http://www.cnet.com/Content/Reviews/Compare/Search/

- **Understanding and Comparing Search Engines -**
  http://www.hamline.edu/library/bush/handouts/comparisons.html

- **How to Search the Web: A Guide to Search Tools -**
  http://issfw.palomar.edu/Library/TGSEARCH.HTM

PRACTICE

Now try a search for your own research topic, using one of the search engines. As you do your search, compare the process to using a subject directory, such as Yahoo.

Your topic: _____

Your keywords or phrases for your search: _____

_____

Search index used: _____

List one good result of your search, including identifying information. URL: _____

Title, name of author or publisher of site, and title:

_____

_____

Describe the value of the online resource you found for your research. Apply appropriate evaluative criteria.

_____

_____

_____

How did the resource compare to your subject directory search? Which search was more effective? Why?

_____

_____

_____

_____

LESSON FIVE:
ALL THE "NEWS"

"Advertisements contain
the only truths to be relied on in a
newspaper."
—Mark Twain

"It's amazing that the amount of
news that happens in the world
every day always just exactly fits
the newspaper."
—Jerry Seinfeld

"The man who reads nothing
at all is better educated than
the man who reads nothing
but newspapers."
—Thomas Jefferson

We all know what the news is: the latest breaking happenings, what everybody is talking about. But the news is fleeting. As Andy Warhol said, everyone has "15 minutes of fame," and today's news is tomorrow's recycling.

Yet staying current with the news is part of being an educated and aware person, an essential element for a critical thinker. In today's rapidly changing world, it is important to be able critically to evaluate information sources while remaining aware of our own cultural assumptions.

CONCEPTS

This lesson addresses these critical thinking skills:

⟹ Differentiate between fact and opinion.
⟹ Examine the assumptions, including your own.
⟹ Be flexible and open minded as you look for explanations, causes, and solutions to problems.
⟹ Be aware of fallacious arguments, ambiguity, and manipulative reasoning.
⟹ Look for reputable sources.

News from today, fresh off the electronic wires via the Internet—that's how to stay informed. Or is it?

Today's news consumer has learned that staying informed by consulting only one source of information limits his knowledge of world events. Most of us are aware of the way the media can present the news with any slant, or angle, it wants. We have learned to be cynical about what the media presents.

Looking for alternative answers or approaches to a problem or situation is part of thinking critically. And accepting only one interpretation of a newsworthy event is not necessarily getting a look at the whole picture. It takes a bit of mental exertion to look beyond the first layer of information. Your exercise in this lesson will be to look at the news from a few different perspectives, to look for background information, and to analyze the sources.

TOOLS

NEWSPAPERS AND MAGAZINES ONLINE

Increasingly, newspapers are becoming available online. "Zines," or Web-based magazines, are also proliferating. You can locate some good sites by using the following resources:

- **CNN Interactive** has to-the-minute news, politics, weather, style, technology, business, and showbiz, including downloadable images, audio, and quicktime movies: **http://www.cnn.com**

- **Ecola Newsstand** includes 3,000 links to periodicals that are maintained by paper-printed newspapers and magazines, with actively updated English language content and unrestricted access: **http://www.ecola.com/news/**

- **Newslink** is produced by the American Journalism Review with links to home pages of newspapers, magazines, TV stations, and radio stations: **http://www.newslink.org/**

Your next exercise has you looking for the latest "hot" topics online. You won't be limited to finding reliable information, but will instead try to follow a newsworthy story through a few different online perspectives. Follow the example shown here; then you will have a chance to do your own.

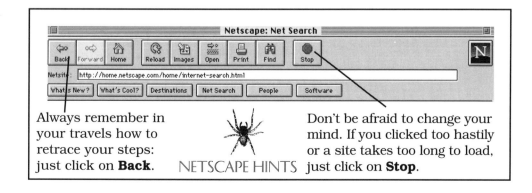

Always remember in your travels how to retrace your steps: just click on **Back**.

NETSCAPE HINTS

Don't be afraid to change your mind. If you clicked too hastily or a site takes too long to load, just click on **Stop**.

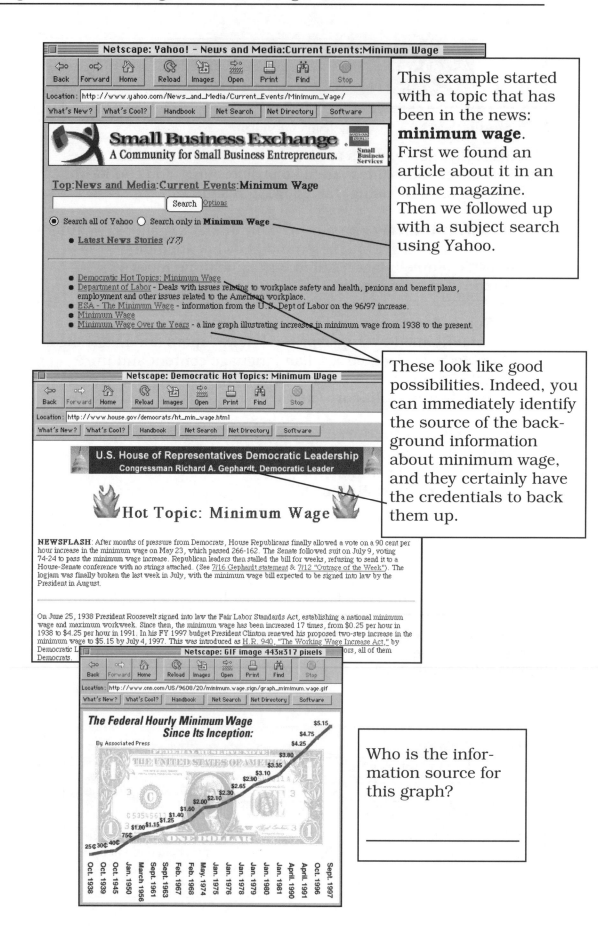

This example started with a topic that has been in the news: **minimum wage**. First we found an article about it in an online magazine. Then we followed up with a subject search using Yahoo.

These look like good possibilities. Indeed, you can immediately identify the source of the background information about minimum wage, and they certainly have the credentials to back them up.

Who is the information source for this graph?

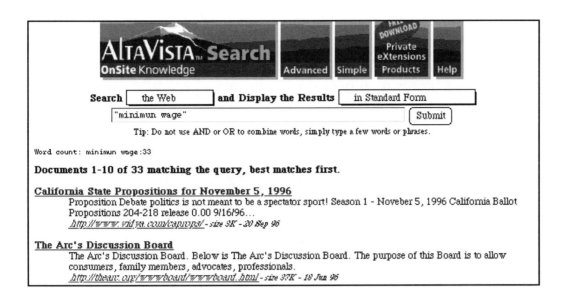

Next, we used the search engine AltaVista to locate additional background information. Remember, AltaVista indexes over 20 million sites, but the search engine does not screen any. The search term **minimum wage** produced the list of hits shown in the preceding illustration. Notice that the results show only 33 hits, which is an amazingly small number considering the topic and the scope of AltaVista. Can you see why? Look closely!

If you followed us on this search, you'll see that all 33 sites made the same mistake we did—they mispelled the word **minimum**. These are good examples to examine for the source's authority, credentials, and reason for showing up on our results list. If you did arrive at this page with us, make a few notes of what you think the value of these resources are.

This exercise has two steps:

1. Examine the current print newspapers for a major news story. Using one of the resources just listed for locating online newspapers, see whether you can find an online news story on the same topic. Compare the news coverage in the print and the online version.

_____

_____

_____

2. Now go for an online search for background information on your news story. You can follow the subject guide approach by using Yahoo or one of the other subject directories, or you can use a general search engine. Describe some of the background information that you discovered. How did it differ from the news articles, both print and online? Did you find any credible background resources? What were they? Did you find some less than valuable resources? Were you able to locate their credits?

_____

_____

_____

_____

_____

_____

LESSON SIX :
LEARNING ON THE WEB

Cliff Stoll, network security expert and author of *Silicon Snake Oil*, says he's "concerned that for all of the online wonders, there is damned little content online. Very little of what I see online has any value, other than as juvenile entertainment" (Stoll 85).

Many people think that there is little of real value on the Web. The Web, due to its lack of a governing structure, ease of online publishing, and unrestricted access has become a smorgasborg of content, from refuse to real meat. In this lesson, you will explore some of the more valuable online material, much of it in the areas of government and education. Some of this content actually is more easily accessible via the Internet than it was in any previous print form. Your online explorations will help build your critical thinking abilities and will emphasize the skills listed below.

⟹ Differentiate between fact and opinion.
⟹ Be flexible and open minded as you look for explanations, causes, and solutions to problems.
⟹ Be aware of fallacious arguments, ambiguity, and manipulative reasoning.
⟹ Look for reputable sources.

It shall be each citizen's personal responsibility to actively pursue needed resources, to recognize when information is needed, and to be able to find, evaluate, and effectively use information (EDUCOM 2).

This statement is part of EDUCOM's Educational Uses of Information Technology, now affiliated with the American Association of Higher Education (AAHE). The statement goes on to cover such very important areas as privacy, freedom of speech, and equal access to technology.

Learning on the Web requires finding resources of value. Many people, like those involved with EDUCOM, feel that learning is an essential responsibility of the electronic community.

CONCEPTS

Your journey onto the Web in this lesson will bring you to many resources. Your quest is for valuable content. You must use your critical thinking skills to stay informed by using credible sources in the online world.

Information professionals (librarians) practice the art of evaluating sources when they develop collections of materials, or libraries. The resources on the Internet are a different matter, however, in that they do not regularly undergo the selection and review process books do before they arrive in your local library. Librarians have tried to identify the features and attributes they use when they determine which materials should be included in a library and which don't belong. Obviously, the decision is not a matter of point of view or taste (excepting items of outstanding "poor taste"). Libraries seek good examples of all points of view for the contribution they will make to the general knowledge, understanding, and enjoyment of the user.

We can approach the resources available online in a similar manner. Each of us individually will be equipped with the evaluation criteria to select items of value to us. In Lesson Two, we gave you some criteria to look for when considering the credibility of an author or publisher. Generally, when you look at books you need to consider the following issues:

- Format – the form in which the information is presented.
- Scope – how extensively the information is covered
- Relation to other works – its relevancy to other works in the same field, reflecting how it builds upon the discipline's body of knowledge
- Authority – the credentials of the author and the reliability or veracity of the source of the information
- Treatment – the level at which the information is presented; for example, scholarly, popular, juvenile, or entertainment only
- Arrangement– how clearly and cohesively the information is presented
- Cost – does the value justify the price?

However, online publishing differs when you consider these items:

- Cost – marketability is not a factor in getting online materials published
- Comprehensiveness – individual online pages rely on hypertext links to provide scope
- Authority – the user must look carefully for statements of responsibility
- Currency – online does not mean up-to-date
- Design and layout of the information – these factors can easily overwhelm or disguise the content

TOOLS

BEST OF THE WEB

In a library, you will find information in book and media form that has been evaluated and selected to be of the greatest value to you. A similar phenomenon is happening online. To guide the user through all the fluff or trash (depending on your level of cynicism) best-of-the-Web sites have been established.

Search engines try to index the over 50 million online pages. Subject directories try to lend some order to a fraction of these pages. In order to cut to the most valuable content available, knowledgeable Web raters use the criteria we just gave you to select what they feel are the "best" sites worth visiting. The number of Web sites included in these "Best of the Web" sites range from a few hundred to around 50,000.

What follows is the "best" of the "Best of the Web" sites, done by *Internet World* in their January 1997 issue. Keep in mind, as a critical thinker, that the preselection of the sites included in these resources is a form of limitation, or subtle guidance, or even censorship, according to what the selectors think is good or valuable. You can—and as you become a practiced "surfer" most likely will—establish your own favorite, or cool, sites, such as these:

- **C/Net Best of the Web** includes 500 reviews engaging their own form of "hipness":
  http://www.cnet.com/

- **Excite Reviews** has the largest selection of rated sites (60,000) using standard and usable subject headings:
  http://www.excite.com/Reviews

- **Lycos Top 5% Sites** was considered the best by *Internet World*:
  http://point.lycos.com

- **Magellan Internet Guide** includes 40,000 sites:
  http://www.mckinley.com

- **NetGuide Live's Best of the Web** stresses online events:
  http://www.netguide.com

- **Yahoo Internet Life Reviews** is limited to only 2,000 sites:
  http://www3.zdnet.com/yil/

PRACTICE

Researching on the Web requires using the best sources. Now that you know how to reach the "Best of the Web," you can do a search that goes straight to the theme of this lesson—education and government.

The Internet is chock full of excellent resources supplied by the government and educational institutions. Indeed, the Internet was initially developed by the federal government in partnership with research and academic institutions. Free public access to government information is a philosophy and requirement of the Internet.

Using Lycos Top 5% Sites at **http://point.lycos.com,** this example searched for **affirmative action in the schools**. By using a "Best of the Web" resource, the intention was to zero in quickly on the most meaty, or high content, areas of education and law. By browsing the subject offerings of Lycos, we selected the categories of **Government** and **Education**.

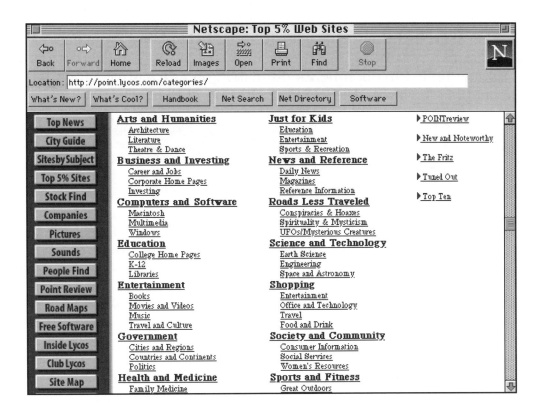

The example followed the Government subject category in search of federal legislation and current laws in Congress concerning affirmative action. This led to Thomas at **http://thomas.loc.gov**, an online federal index to bills in Congress.

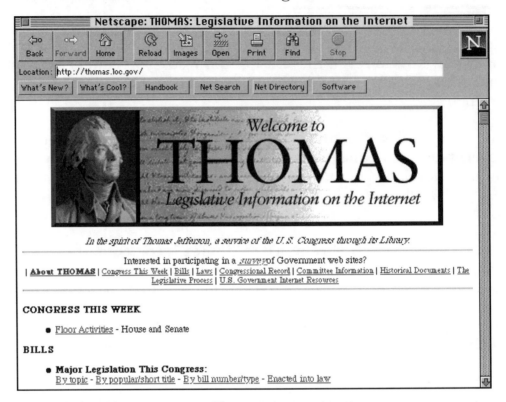

We also searched the U.S. Code online at **http://law.house.gov/usc.htm** before turning to Education. Visiting the U.S. Department of Education led to documents published on affirmative action in the field of education. Here is the selection of results:

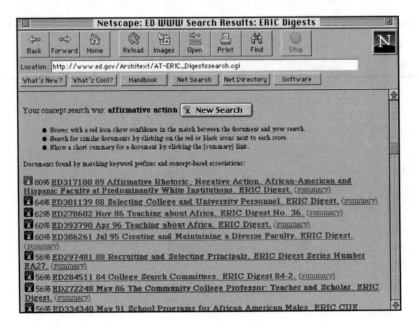

The next lead went to ERIC—an educational research bibliographic database of over 850,000 conference papers, reports, instructional materials, research articles, and other materials, in print, on CD-ROM, and now online. ERIC can be searched through **AskERIC** at **http://ericir.syr.edu/** or through other sites at **http://ericae2.educ.cua.edu/search.htm**.

No self-respecting researcher can miss the opportunity to search the table of contents of 17,000 journals by keyword and to order online full-text article delivery through **Uncover - http://uncweb.carl.org/**

The online search for affirmative action could have stopped right there, but we skipped ahead and visited a site that specializes in political issues. Here's what we found at **AZ Connect: For Your Information - http://www.getnet.com:80/azconnect/fyi.html:**

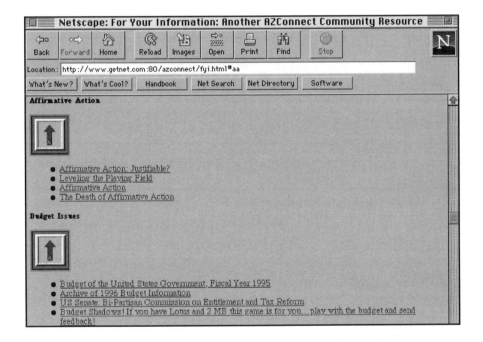

This completed our online researching. Now you pick a topic to explore in government and education resources, following the learning theme of this lesson. Select one of the "Best of the Web" sites as a starting point. Look for the best content; you should find plenty of it!

For this exercise, you do not need to pick a specific subject to research in advance. Just select one of the "Best of the Web" sites and try to find your way into some government information. Look for categories such as Government, Federal, Legislation, Politics, Agencies, etc. Once you find the site, follow your own intuition. Go until you find some useful or interesting content. You are creating your own research topic.

Where did you end up? Give the URL and the name of government agency or issuing body of the information. Give the title of the document or resource you found, and explain its research value.

_____

_____

_____

_____

_____

Now it is time to switch gears and steer in the educational direction. You may want to go back to the "Best of the Web" site you just used, or try using ERIC or Uncover, as described in the preceding practice. Either way, your mission is to discover educational journal articles or documents on the same topic you just explored through government agencies. Describe what you found, tell whether and how it relates to your research topic, and give its overall research value.

_____

_____

_____

_____

_____

TOOLS

The voices emanating from the Web are a social and cultural cacophony. You can find most any opinion and point of view espoused on the Internet. By virtue of its self-publishing nature, the Internet harkens back to the pamphlets and public flyers of the days of the American Revolution.

Let's tune in to the public's voice now on the Internet to explore some of the political issues and controversies of today's voters.

Here are an assortment of sites. Visit one and find an issue. Be a critical thinker. Look at the information there with the goal of becoming informed, seeking alternative viewpoints, and keeping an open mind.

- **AZ Connect: For Your Information** has links to information on public issues:
  http://www.getnet.com:80/azconnect/fyi.html

- **Jefferson Project** claims to be the most complete archive of political resources today:
  http://www.voxpop.org/jefferson/

- **Vote Smart Web** is a new service made available by Project Vote Smart, a nonprofit organization. Project Vote Smart's database is available with other sources of political information found on the Internet and is researcher-assisted via an 800 number. Links include the 1996 presidential campaign, issues, organizations, educational reference materials, and other directories of political information:
  http://www.vote-smart.org/

- **Vote Smart Web** also includes Individual Issues in depth, from a wide range of Internet sources:
  http://www.vote-smart.org/issues/

- **Welcome to the Campaign Central Home Page** has the top political topics of the day, with links to background information, government resources, nonprofit and political associations' home pages:
  http://www.clark.net/ccentral/

PRACTICE

Select one of the sites which covers today's politics and controversial topics. Travel far enough into the site to locate a piece of information that carries an identifiable point of view. Read briefly through it, and report what you find.

What is the source of the political information that you found?

_____

_____

Citing electronic sources is different from citing print sources, but the pieces of information you need for a citation are similar. Lesson Eight will explain the basic format for citing electronic sources. When you need to do extensive citations of electronic documents, make sure that you review one of the up-to-date style manuals listed in Lesson Eight.

For now, cite what you found by listing the pertinent information: author, issuing agency (publisher), date, page, and URL.

_____

_____

Critically evaluate the source. What is the opinion of the author or issuing agency? How comprehensively is the information presented? Does the document do a good job presenting that point of view? Can you identify the assumptions or biases of the author? Give an example.

_____

_____

_____

_____

_____

LESSON SEVEN:
PEOPLE ARE TALKING

"I think there is a world market for maybe five computers." — Thomas Watson, chairman of IBM, 1943

"I have traveled the length and breadth of this country and talked with the best people, and I can assure you that data processing is a fad that won't last out the year." — The editor in charge of business books for Prentice Hall, 1957

"There is no reason anyone would want a computer in their home." — Ken Olson, president, chairman and founder of Digital Equipment Corp., 1977

"But what . . . is it good for?" — Engineer at the Advanced Computing Systems Division of IBM, 1968, commenting on the microchip

"Computers in the future may weigh no more than 1.5 tons." — *Popular Mechanics*, 1949, forecasting the relentless march of science

(Hertig 1)

These quotes show what people were saying about computers yesterday. What are they saying now? Similarly ridiculous assertions and prognostications of the future? This lesson explores the answer to that question.

One of the most amazing and liberating contributions of the Internet is the ability to communicate, almost instantaneously, with anyone, anywhere the Internet reaches. By using electronic mail (e-mail), you can communicate in seconds to friends, colleagues, peers, and experts, provided that you have, or can locate, their e-mail addresses.

A journey out into the virtual community will introduce you to electronic communication, tools to locate people, and a comparison of the real and the virtual worlds of communication.

In this lesson you will practice the following critical thinking skills:

> ⇒ Differentiate between fact and opinion.
> ⇒ Examine assumptions, including your own.
> ⇒ Be aware of fallacious arguments, ambiguity, and manipulative reasoning.
> ⇒ Stay focused on the whole picture, while examining the specifics.

CONCEPTS

Just what is the virtual community? This phenomenon is worth studying, and for the duration of this lesson you will be learning about the members of this virtual community and discovering what they are talking about.

"A new world is arising in the vast web of digital, electronic media which connect us. Computer-based communications media like electronic mail and computer conferencing are becoming the basis of new forms of community. These communities without a single, fixed geographical location comprise the first settlements on an electronic frontier. Digital networks offer a tremendous potential to empower individuals in an over-powering world. However, these communication networks are also the subject of significant debate concerning governance and freedom." — Electronic Frontier Foundation, 1996

Who is on the Internet? We know the number of Internet users is growing dramatically, some say 15 percent per month. But who will we hear talking out there? The following statistics are drawn from recent surveys of Internet users published in the December 1996 issue of *Internet World.*

Number of U.S. users:	from 23 to 42 million
Average age:	33 years old
Women:	31.5%
Men:	68.5%
Average annual income:	$59,000
Occupation:	
Education related	30%
Computer related	27.8%
Professional	18.9%
Management	10.7%
Politics:	
Democrat or Independent/ Democrat	41.8%
Republican or Independent/ Republican	31.4%

(Kantor and Neubarth, 1996)

DEFINITIONS

Mailing lists, or electronic discussion groups, are groups of people with similar interests who communicate electronically on selected subjects. The process by which the discussion is managed and the commands you use vary depending on the mail server program the host computer is using (for example, Listserv, Listproc, Mailbase, Mailserv, or Majordomo).

Generally referred to simply as **listservs**, mailing lists allow anyone on the Internet with electronic mail access to subscribe. A message posted to a listserv is received by all other subscribers to the list. These discussion groups can be listened to (a process called *lurking*), or contributed to, provided that you follow the general theme and are not offensive or disrespectful to fellow subscribers (which is known as *flaming*). "Netiquette" is a general term for the personal and communication protocol that is expected to regulate electronic behavior. Some good online resources on netiquette are these:

- "The Net: User Guidelines and Netiquette" by Arlene H. Rinaldi
  http://www.fau.edu/rinaldi/net/index.htm

- "Netiquette" by Chuq Von Rospach and Gene Spafford
  http://redtail.unm.edu/cp/netiquette.html

Mailing lists provide two basic functions: (1) they give users the ability to distribute a message to a group of people by sending it to a single, central address, and (2) the ability to join and leave the list at any time. You need to remember, however, that these are two different functions, with two different e-mail addresses. First, the "listname address" is the address you use to send any messages that you intend to be read by the list subscribers. Second, the "administrative address" is the address to which you send any commands or requests that affect your subscription to the list.

These exercises will not ask you to go through the process of joining a mailing list, but you will get a job aid (a handy list of the basic procedures) for your future use. The practice will involve the discovery of the range and diversity of mailing lists and show you how to find topics that interest you. For further information on listservs and e-mail, try these sites:

http://www.clark.net/pub/lschank/explore/email.html
http://www.lsoft.com/manuals/user/user.html

Listserv is a broadly used mailing list program. Here are steps
to follow for subscribing:

---

1. Open a new mail message.
2. In the **To:** line, enter the administration e-mail address of the
   listserv you wish to join.
3. Leave the **Subject** line blank.
4. In the message area enter the word subscribe, the name of
   the listserv, and your name.
5. Send the message.

EXAMPLE: To subscribe to a listserv called "equis," Jamie Jones
would do the following:

    Mail to: listserv@uauvm.ua.edu
    Subject:
    Message:subscribe equis Jamie Jones.

However, to post a message to the "equis" listserv:

    Mail to: equis@uauvm.ua.edu
    Subject: *Type briefly what your message is about.*
    Message: *Type your message.*

Joining a listserv is an easy process, although the exact commands
vary for the different types of mailing lists. The basic commands to
subscribe are often included in indexes of mailing lists, with further commands available online after you have subscribed. For this
exercise, look through the indexes and directories given here and
locate two mailing lists that you would like to join. To actually
subscribe, you need to have established an e-mail account.

In this exercise, you will visit one of these sites to find an interesting mailing list. Examples of sample searches are given. For your
search, think of some keywords describing a topic of interest or
area of research.

TOOLS

LISTSERV DIRECTORIES

This example uses two directories of e-mail discussion groups to locate listservs on the topic of "critical thinking." The first one is

http://www.liszt.com/

Here are the results of the search:

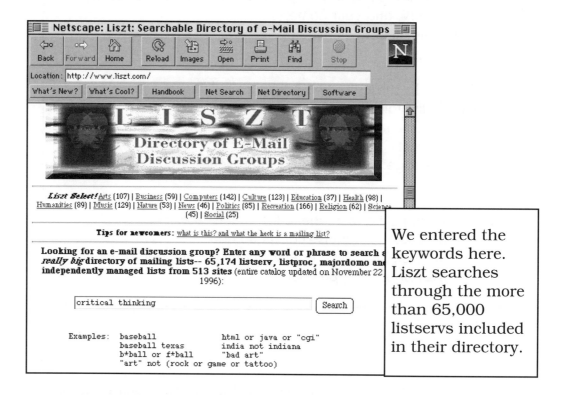

We entered the keywords here. Liszt searches through the more than 65,000 listservs included in their directory.

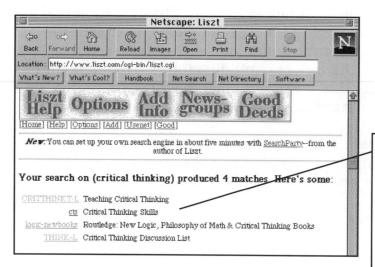

This shows results of the search. Click on any of the results to get the e-mail address to subscribe.

TOOLS

LISTSERV DIRECTORIES

The second search uses Tile.Net. The URL is:

http://tile.net/lists/

Note: Sometimes the URL you enter differs from what the location shows. Many sites have multiple addresses or URLs.

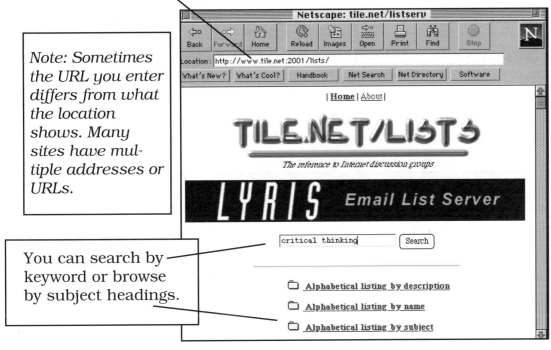

You can search by keyword or browse by subject headings.

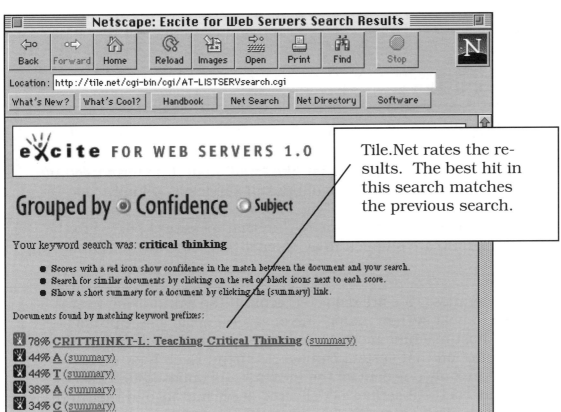

Tile.Net rates the results. The best hit in this search matches the previous search.

PRACTICE

LOCATING LISTSERVS

Now give the results of your search for listservs.

Which site or sites did you use? What did you find? Name the listservs that looked most interesting to you. If you used both sites for searching, which did you prefer?

_____

_____

_____

_____

_____

_____

_____

CONCEPTS

USENET

Electronic mail (e-mail), just like "snail mail" (the term used by Net folk to describe the usual postal service) is usually "one-to-one." That is, one piece of mail goes to one person. Usenet communication is "many-to-many," in that messages posted to the newsgroup are shipped to all Usenet host machines around the world.

Usenet messages are delivered around the world, from host system to host system, using one of several specific Net protocols. The host machine receives the messages and everybody with an account on that system can access them. Each host system has to store only one copy of the message, as opposed to listservs, where each subscriber is delivered every message to their individual e-mail account.

Over 15,000 newsgroups exist in different languages, covering an immense range of topics. Newsgroup names start with one of a series of broad topic names, which are usually self-evident. For example, newsgroups beginning with "comp" are about particular computer-related topics. Some host systems present you with the broad range of newgroup topic areas and other systems let you compile your own "reading list" so that you only see messages in the newsgroup you want.

MAJOR USENET HIERARCHY CATEGORIES

alt	"Alternative" topics
comp	Computer hardware and software
misc	Topics that don't fit anywhere else
news	Groups that deal with Usenet issues
rec	Recreational subjects and hobbies
sci	Topics in the established sciences
soc	Groups for discussing social issues and socializing
talk	Lengthy discussions and debates

Usenet newsgroups can provide an interesting way to tune into the hot topics on people's minds, giving you a global perspective. Consider newsgroup discussions as a sort of online talk radio, minus the moderator, or like an international graffiti wall.

Amazing numbers of words are being tossed around via newsgroups. An average day may see 800 megabytes of Usenet postings, which is equal to 800 400-page novels (DejaNews, 1997). As the following example shows, Usenet messages come in a large range of sources.

You can use newsgroup archives to follow threads of discussion and research what people have said concerning certain topics. This exercise will allow you to tap into this goldmine of information. But remember, as critical thinkers, information can come from many different sources, print or nonprint, but in all cases, you must consider the source and its validity and point of view. More information about Usenet newsgroups is available at these sites:

http://ancho.ucs.indiana.edu/NetRsc/usenet.html

http://dejanews.com/help/dnusenet_help.html

TOOLS

This practice exercise explores Usenet newsgroups by using their archives. A few easy search engines are available to access the archives of recent newsgroups articles. You can follow this sample search; then try your own. The search engines you will use are:

- **DejaNews - http://www.dejanews.com/**
  DejaNews is a Usenet archiving and searching service that keeps all the Usenet messages that have been posted and provides an easy searchable interface.

- **AltaVista - http://www.altavista.digital.com/**
  and
- **Infoseek - http://www.infoseek.com/**
  These all-purpose search engines allow you to enter your key search terms and then elect to search only through the newgroups archives (Usenet), not all of the Web.

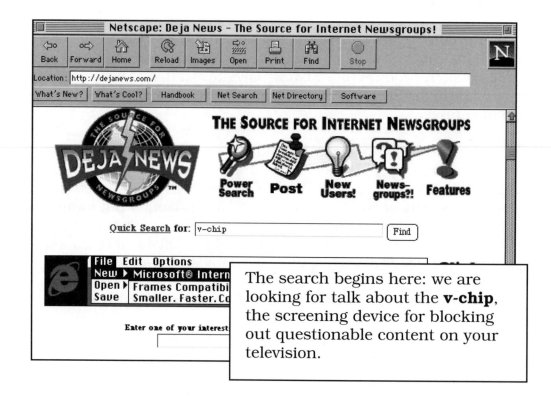

The search begins here: we are looking for talk about the **v-chip**, the screening device for blocking out questionable content on your television.

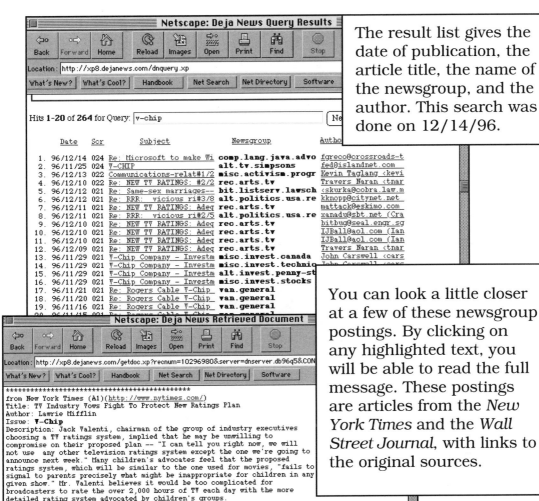

The result list gives the date of publication, the article title, the name of the newsgroup, and the author. This search was done on 12/14/96.

You can look a little closer at a few of these newsgroup postings. By clicking on any highlighted text, you will be able to read the full message. These postings are articles from the *New York Times* and the *Wall Street Journal*, with links to the original sources.

Here is a selection from a presidential news conference given just a day ago. These can be directly accessed through **http://www.whitehouse.gov**

>You ever hear of the **V-CHIP**? That's one of Mr. Clinton's pet projects.

      Actually, the "**V-chip**" is an EXCELLENT way for society to
PROTECT its freedoms of expression. With that, the TV producers
can have open season in a full range of subjects. The
goody-two-shoes types can simply program their V-chips to filter
out what they don't want to see, while the rest of us can enjoy
better and more versatile programming than ever. I'm all for it!
The **V-chip** is a virtual guarantee of the END of censorship!

>Actually I see nothing wrong with pressuring businesses to stop selling and
>distributing materials that are harmful to our nation.

      Nothing is more harmful to our nation than eroding our
freedom of speech, press, and expression. If we ever lost those,
we can see the ultimate outcome by remembering what happened to
the Chinese freedom-fighters in Tianenmen Square. Just because a
few wackoes misuse porography, for example, is no reason to wreck
our freedoms. Driving 65 and up, as allowed by law by the
states, permits many more deaths than would a national speed
limit of 15 mph. We know that the latter is ludicrous, and would
wreck the country. So would censorship.

And here is a selection from another Usenet message on the topic.

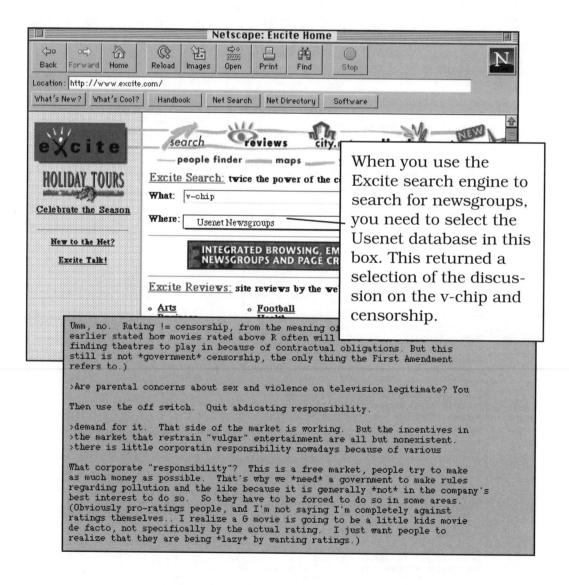

When you use the Excite search engine to search for newsgroups, you need to select the Usenet database in this box. This returned a selection of the discussion on the v-chip and censorship.

You might feel, after reading through a few of these newsgroup messages, that you just dropped in on multi-faceted discussions in progress. Did you discern any examples of the writer's opinions, illogical reasoning, or unsupported analogies or claims? Give specific examples.

_____

_____

_____

_____

_____

PRACTICE

Now it's your turn. Remember that, as a critical thinker, it is your task to stay focused on your research question and to keep an open mind. Choose either DejaNews or Excite to search for newsgroup articles about your research interests. Read enough of the articles you locate to get a feel for the threads in the discussion. Then list some examples of the discussion and arguments you found.

_____

_____

_____

_____

_____

_____

CONCEPTS

FINDING SOMEONE ON THE NET

Finding someone's e-mail address isn't as simple as it might seem. Often it is said that the best way to get someone's e-mail address is just to ask him or her. If asking is not a feasible option, however, you need to know about a few of the search tools available on the Internet, how to get to them, and what to expect.

A few of these "white pages" directories have been incorporated into the larger search engines, making it much easier and faster to access the best possibilities. You'll find some of the meta-search engines include options for people searches. This exercise lists some of the current search engines offering "white pages" searching.

TOOLS

- **Switchboard-**
  http://www.switchboard.com/

- **WhoWhere? PeopleSearch-**
  http://www.whowhere.com/

- **Yahoo! People Search-**
  http://www.yahoo.com/search/people/

- **PeopleSearch**
  http://www.w3com.com/psearch/

- **Internet Address Finder**
  http://www.iaf.net/

- **People Search (US)**
  http://206.129.166.101/people.html

- **Four11 White Page Directory**
  http://www.four11.com/

- **Lycos**
  http://www.lycos.com/pplfndr.html

Now is your turn to be an evaluator. All of the search engines listed on the previous page do basically the same thing: find people. Yet each of them may draw from a different database. Select two to compare. Explore each site long enough to find out about its resources: how does it get its information, how comprehensive and up-to-date is it, who would you likely to find in its directories? Then select a name to search in each engine—someone you know who has an e-mail address, a relative, or someone famous, or maybe yourself. Describe your results below.

List the two "people search" directories you used:

_____

_____

Where did each one get its information?

_____

_____

How were they the same? How were they different?

_____

_____

Who would you be likely to find using each directory?

_____

_____

Who did you look for? Were you able to locate the person?

_____

_____

Why or why not?

_____

_____

LESSON EIGHT: SPINNING YOUR WEB

> "A virtual community is a set of on-going, many-sided interactions that occur predominantly in and through computers linked via telecommunications networks. They are a fairly recent phenomena and one that is rapidly developing as more people come to have access to computers and data networks. The virtual spaces constructed by these technologies are not only new, they have some fundamental differences from more familiar terrain of interaction. Virtual spaces change the kinds of communication that can be exchanged between individuals and alter the economies of communication and organization."
> (Smith 2)

You have reached your last lesson. As a critical thinker, you will be given just a few more tools to make the journey through the world of Internet information a little easier. Each of these tools will help you make your voice heard in the online world.

This course has introduced you to the idea of an electronic community. You have seen some of what you might expect to find in this online world and learned how to go about locating what you need. By now you realize that the Web is changing quickly and that new technologies and tools are emerging every day.

The true art of being a critical thinker is flexibility. Being able to adjust, refocus, try a new tactic to a difficult problem, or simply stand back and withhold judgement all require flexibility. You will no doubt become proficient with any number of tools in your chosen world, whether they are thinking and communicating skills, or the more concrete tools and skills required in any profession or life endeavor. Whatever level of proficiency you attain, the ability to stay flexible and think critically will be your most valuable tool.

CONCEPTS

Using your computer for e-mail or researching on the Internet requires the art and policy of respecting certain restrained and polite modes of behavior. Various sites offer Netiquette rules, as listed on page 66. The following "commandments" point out other areas of cultural behavior of which you should be aware.

THE TEN COMMANDMENTS FOR COMPUTER ETHICS
from the Computer Ethics Institute

1. Thou shalt not use a computer to harm other people.

2. Thou shalt not interfere with other people's computer work.

3. Thou shalt not snoop around in other people's files.

4. Thou shalt not use a computer to steal.

5. Thou shalt not use a computer to bear false witness.

6. Thou shalt not use or copy software for which you have not paid.

7. Thou shalt not use other people's computer resources without authorization.

8. Thou shalt not appropriate other people's intellectual output.

9. Thou shalt think about the social consequences of the program you write.

10. Thou shalt use a computer in ways that show consideration and respect.

You can access this list on the Web at this URL:
http://www.fau.edu/rinaldi/net/ten.html

TOOLS

Researching on the Web will require that you become familiar with the proper format for citing electronic sources. Many style manuals have not completely caught up with the nuances of citations for online references. In fact, most of the citation style guides we examined varied considerably, both for APA and MLA format. Below are some general examples, in MLA format. On the following page, you will find some selected electronic citation sources.

BIBLIOGRAPHIC CITATIONS

General Rule

Author's Last Name, First Name. "Title of Work." "Title of Complete Work" (if applicable). Document date or last revision (if different from access date. Protocol and address, access path or directories (date of access).

Listserv Messages

Hertig, Linda [linda_hertig@ISR.SYR.EDU]. "Famous last words." THINK-L@UMSLVMA.UMSL.EDU. (12 Oct. 1995).

World Wide Web

Janicke, Lisa. "Resource Selection and Information Evaluation." http://alexia.lis.uiuc.edu/~janicke/Evaluate.html. (6 June 1996).

Gopher Site

EDUCOM. "Bill of Rights and Responsibilities for Electronic Learners." gopher://abacus.bates.edu:70/00/. (August 1993).

FTP Site

EDUCOM. "Bill of Rights and Responsibilities for Electronic Learners." August 1993. ftp://ftp.american.edu. (7 Sept. 1996).

Personal E-mail

Griffin, Laura. "Electronic confusion." Personal e-mail. (31 July, 1995).

SELECTED ELECTRONIC CITATIONS SOURCES

Use these sources to find out more about electronic citations:

A Brief Citation Guide for Internet Sources in History and the
Humanities
http://www.nmmc.com/libweb/employee/citguide.htm

Classroom Connect: How to Cite Internet Resources
**http://www.classroom.net/classroom/
CitingNetResources.html**

Bibliographic Formats for Citing Electronic Information
http://www.arsc.sunyit.edu/~com400/estyles.htm

Walker, Janice, Univ. of South Florida (MLA Style)
http://www.cas.usf.edu/english/walker/mla.html

COPYRIGHT NOTICE

> This document may be linked to, downloaded, printed, or copied for noncommercial use without further permission of the author, provided that the content is not modified and this statement appears at the bottom of the page. Any use not stated above requires the written consent of the author.

You might have noticed statements such as this one appearing on the bottom of Web pages. You might also have discovered how easy it is to copy Web pages. You can copy pages by opening the File menu and choosing **Save As** and then choosing **Format Text** or by simply using the copy and paste text editing tools. Issues of copyright are being debated furiously on the Web and in the courts. Respecting copyright and intellectual property remains basically the same in print or online. **It is best to assume that anything you find on the Internet is protected by copyright. Be careful not to misuse the apparently "free" materials on the Web, and always cite fully the resources you use.**

TOOLS

HOOKING UP TO THE INTERNET

Throughout this book, you have learned a lot about how to visit the Web, how to find what you're interested in, and how to evaluate what you find. But at some point, you might want to take a more active role by accessing the Internet directly from your home and by starting to publish on the Web.

To connect to the Internet from your home you need a personal computer (IBM compatible with Windows or a Macintosh of a Quadra level or higher), a modem, communications software, and a phone line. Your modem should be at least a 14.4 bps (most people now are using a 28.8 or 33.6 modem). The speed of the modem controls the time it takes to download images and text off the Internet. Too slow a modem will turn the World Wide Web into the World Wide Wait.

Unless you have Internet access through your school or work, you will need to go through a commercial Internet service provider for your connection. The business of Internet service providers is highly competitive, and the range of services varies.

Some sites on the Web provide national directories of Internet service providers. Here are a few:

- The List: 4,176 Internet Service Providers and Growing!
  http://thelist.iworld.com/

- POICA: Providers of Commercial Internet Access
  http://www.celestin.com/pocia/

- ISP Finder
  http://www.ispfinder.com/

TOOLS

WRITING HTML

After you have surfed the Web for a while, you might get the itch to try electronic publishing yourself. HTML is certainly easy enough to learn, and most browsers allow you to save Web pages by HTML source code, revealing the hypertext information. (The latest versions of Netscape even include an HTML editing application.) To save a hypertext page in the source file mode, all you have to do is open the File menu and choose **Save as**.

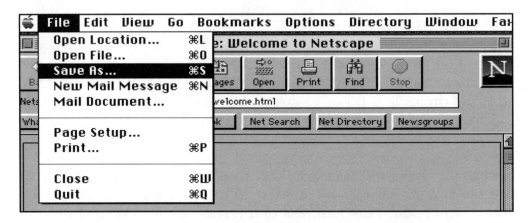

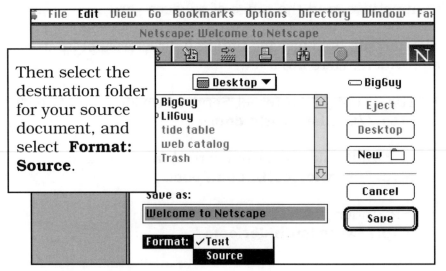

Then select the destination folder for your source document, and select **Format: Source**.

To view a Web page you have created in HTML, you don't need to have posted it on an Internet server. You can save it as a file locally (on your own computer), start Netscape, open the File menu, select **Open File**, locate your file, and see how your page might look to the online world.

Now that you are an experienced Web searcher, you will have no trouble locating resources to instruct you how to create HTML. There are HTML style manuals, tutorials, documents of rules and standards, and free HTML editing software all available on the Web. Here are two good resources to get you started:

- HTML Crash Course for Educators by Andy Carvin complete with interactive HTML quizzes.
  http://edweb.cnidr.org:90/htmlintro.html

- The NCSA Beginner's Guide to HTML. The guide is used by many to start to understand HTML.
  http://www.ncsa.uiuc.edu/General/Internet/WWW/

CONCEPTS

HTML PUBLISHING

Once you have surfed the Net a fair amount, you will no doubt find that critical thinking is often lacking on the Web. Most people agree that part of the problem is the essence of electronic publishing. Anyone with an HTML editor and access to a computer server can publish a home page. No standards or credentials are needed——only a very basic skill level and minimal cost. Just write it and post it.

For this reason we remind all future contributors to electronic publishing to remember three key points of presenting their information on the Web.

- **Seek a clear statement of the question.** Think before you write your pages: what exactly do you intend to say, and what are the questions that you seek to answer by making this information available?
- **Stay relevant to the main point.** It is very easy in hypertext to make connections to anything and all things you find interesting, vaguely related or not. Try to remember that anyone on the Web has access to those same links in any number of different ways, and that your links should be carefully selected and clearly related to the purpose of the information you present.

- **Keep your mind on the whole picture, while dealing with the specifics.** Getting lost in the technical considerations of electronic publishing, the "bells and whistles," is not an uncommon problem on the Web. Remain true to the mission and goal of the publication you are creating and use only the technical extras when they are necessary to support the message of your pages.

PRACTICE

FINAL EXERCISE!

Now it is your turn to practice, free form. You can browse, surf, or consult your favorite search engine or Web index. The quest is for something you would find useful in becoming more knowledgeable about the Internet. Think of some of the topics presented in this book: electronic publishing, virtual communities, netiquette, critical thinking, evaluation of sources, online learning opportunities, or computers and education.

What is your question? This is really the researcher's most difficult question, though it might sound elemental. To be able to state clearly and directly the essence of what you intend to research is no easy matter. You can get lost in your own assumptions about what you think will be found and be confused by what you already believe or know. The researcher has to wade through all these preconceptions and state the most open and succinct research question possible.

What is your question?

Where do you think the best resources for your question will be found? Will the Internet be a useful tool? Why do you feel that way?

_____

_____

_____

_____

_____

_____

Your adventure on the Web has just begun. Good luck!

GLOSSARY/INDEX

Archie - System which allows you to search indexes of public file archives on the Internet by doing a keyword search of anonymous ftp sites.

Browser - A software program that allows you to navigate the Internet and view Web documents, often offering a suite of other applications that perform FTP and multimedia functions.

Client/Server - The model used for many of the popular Internet tools, such as Gopher, WWW, Archie and WAIS. The *server* is the software on the host computer (the one you are accessing from your own computer). A *client* (the computer from which your are working) asks a server to display a file. The server will then "serve up" the data to the client. (see pg. 7)

CWIS - CampusWide Information Systems that provide electronic access, via Gopher or other software, about campus information, such as course schedules, telephone numbers, or publications.

Domain Name - A structured, alphabet-based unique name for a computer on a network, as opposed to the computer's numeric IP (Internet Protocol) name. Either name can be used. For example, 198.15.133.62 or summa.lib.unh.edu (see pg. 8).

Electronic Journals (e-journals) - Full-text journal publications which are available only in electronic form. Like print journals, e-journals cover a wide variety of subjects (see pg. 46).

FAQ (pronounced "fak") - A list of frequently asked questions and their answers. Many newsgroups, along with other lists, maintain such a list so that people won't waste time asking and answering the same questions over and over.

FTP - An acronym for File transfer protocol, FTP is a software program that allows you to transfer files from one computer to another. FTP allows for the transfer of large files very quickly over the Internet.

Gopher - Menu-based software which allows you to navigate across the Internet to access resources. Gopher is a public domain, client/server based software (see pg. 7).

HTML - HyperText Markup Language (HTML) is used to format documents delivered by Web servers using a set of tags that allow you to create and format Web pages and screens. Web screen displays are based on how the Web clients interpret the tags which have been applied to the text (see pg. 15, 80-81).

HTTP - Hypertext Transport Protocol (HTTP) is a protocol that embeds within a document the command and information to allow navigation to other documents on the Internet (see pg. 7).

Hyperlinks - Hyperlinks are the text or images that contains "links" to other documents. Words, phrases, or images in the document that can be chosen by a reader to retrieve and display another document are hyperlinks (see pg. 7).

Internet (the Net) - A worldwide network of computer networks that are connected, using the IP and other protocols, which provide access to electronic mail, remote login, file transfer, and other services (see pg. 5).

IP (Internet Protocol) name - A structured, numeric-based unique name for a computer on a network. The number includes four sections separated by periods. For example, 198.15.133.62 or summa.lib.unh.edu (see pg. 8).

LISTSERV - Subject-oriented electronic mailing list to which anyone on the Internet with electronic mail access may subscribe. A message posted to a listserv is received by all other subscribers to the list. Not all electronic mailing lists use Listserv software, so user commands vary (see pg. 63-67).

Lynx - A text-based client used to access information on the Web. Lynx cannot handle sound, image, graphic, or video files.

Mailing Lists - Electronic discussion groups consisting of people with similar interests who communicate electronically on selected subjects. Mailing lists are managed by different mail server programs (such as Listserv, Listproc, Mailbase, Mailserv, or Majordomo), depending on the host computer (see pg. 63-67).

Mosaic - NCSC Mosaic, the first and—until recently—best known Web browser. This Web client, unlike Lynx, handles multimedia files, including sounds, images, graphics, and moving images. Mosaic requires a fairly high-end computer and a direct, or a SLIP (PPP) connection to the Internet. Mosaic will not run on a standard dial-up modem access.

Netscape - Netscape Navigator, developed by the original programmers of Mosaic, is a popular Web browser, allowing full multimedia functions (see pg. v).

PPP or Point to Point Protocol- The protocol that allows a computer equipped with a standard telephone line and high-speed modem, using TCP/IP (Internet protocols, to become a full Internet member. A computer with a PPP (or SLIP) connection can run graphic browsers such as Mosaic and Netscape and has its own domain name (IP address). PPP is Similar to Slip, or Serial Line Protocol.

Remote Host - The computer or computer network with resources that can be accessed by another computer on the Internet. These hosts are usually accessed via telnet.

TCP/IP or Transmission control protocol/Internet protocol - The protocols that define the standards for how computers talk to each other and thus allow data to pass between the variety of networks which make up the Internet.

Telnet - A "terminal emulation" protocol that allows the user to log in to remote computer systems on the Internet. When you use telnet software, you are using computing resources of the host computer (see pg. 16).

UNIX - Computer operating system which played a key role in the development of the Internet. Unix is case-sensitive and because many machines on the Internet run Unix as their operating system, users often have to be careful to type their log in commands exactly as directed in instructions.

URL - Uniform Resource Locator. A standard method to describe the "address" of a particular resource on the Internet. The section before the colon refers to the access method; the section after the double slashes is the address of the computer where the resource is located, and the last item shows the directory path for that page. For example, http://www.clark.net/pub/lschank/web/learn.html (see pg. 5).

Usenet (also known as "netnews") - An informal group of electronic systems that exchange "news" on a broad range of subjects, similar to bulletin boards on other networks (see pg. 67-69).

Veronica - Very easy rodent-oriented net-wide index to computerized archives or Veronica, performs a keyword search of gopher menus and titles. The search results are displayed via a newly created gopher, based on your search.

VT100 - A standard and probably the most common protocol for terminal emulation used when telnetting to a remote host. VT100 usually does not allow for commands and features that are available with a workstation-based client. (For example, the use of a mouse.) See also *client/server*.

WWW (also known as the "Web" or "W3") - World Wide Web is a global hypermedia-based system which allows access to the universe of Internet resources, text, audio, graphics, and moving image files. This public domain, client/server based software is actually a suite of software, protocols, and conventions which make it easy to browse and contribute to the Internet (see pg. 5, 30).

REFERENCES

Computer Ethics Institute. "The Ten Commandments for Computer Ethics." http://www.fau.edu/rinaldi/net/ten.html. (4 April 96).

DejaNews. "What is Usenet?" http://dejanews.com/dnusenet_help.html. (15 March 1997).

Dewey, John. *How We Think.* Chicago: Regnery, 1933.

EDUCOM. "Bill of Rights and Responsibilities for Electronic Learners." gopher://abacus.bates.edu:70/00/. August 1993.

Ennis, Richard. "A Taxonomy of Critical Thinking Dispositions and Abilities. *Teaching Thinking Skills.* Ed. J. B. Baron and R. J. Sternberg. New York: W.H. Freeman, 1986.

Ennis, Richard, and J. Millman. *Cornell Tests of Critical Thinking.* Pacific Grove, Cal.: Midwest Publications, 1985.

Glaser, Ernest. *An Experiment in the Development of Critical Thinking.* New York: Teachers College of Columbia Univ. Bureau of Publications, 1941.

Hertig, Linda. [linda_hertig@ISR.SYR.EDU]. "Famous Last Words." THINK-L@UMSLVMA.UMSL.EDU. (Oct 12, 1995).

Janicke, Lisa. (janicke@alexia.lis.uiuc.edu). "Resource Selection and Information Evaluation." http://alexia.lis.uiuc.edu/~janicke/Evaluate.html. 1994.

Kantor, Andrew and Michael Neubarth. "Off the Charts: How Big is the Internet?" *Internet World.* December, 1996: 45-51.

Kapor, Mitch. (mkapor@eff.org) "Electronic Frontier Foundation." http://www.eff.org/EFFdocs/about_eff.html. 1996.

Page, Melvin. "Bibliographic Citations." NETTRAIN@UBVM.CC.BUFFALO.EDU. (8 Nov 1995).

Rader, Hannelore, Billie Reinhart and Gary Thompson. *Evaluating Information: A Basic Checklist.* http://www.lib.utc.edu/info.html. 1994.

Scriven, Michael, and Richard Paul. "Three Definitions of Critical Thinking." http://www.sonoma.edu/cthink/definect.html. 1996.

Simon, Herbert. "Managing a Wealth of Digitized Information." *Scientific American* Sept. 1995: 201.

Smith, Linda. "Selection and Evaluation of Reference Sources." *Reference and Information Services: An Introduction.* Ed. Richard E. Bopp and Linda C. Smith. Englewood, CO: Libraries Unlimited, 1991. 240.

Smith Mark A. "The Logic of the Virtual Commons." http://www.sscnet.ucla.edu/soc/csoc/virtcomm.html. 1994.

Stoll, Clifford. "Review." *Computerworld.* Aug. 14, 1995:85.

Venditto, Gus. "Critic's Choice." *Internet World.* January, 1997: 83-96.

Wurman, Richard. *Information Anxiety.* New York: Bantam Books.1989.